A Church of Power Is Emerging

Don Faix

© Copyright 1993 — Don Faix

All rights reserved. This book is protected under the copyright laws of the United States of America. This book may not be copied or reprinted for commercial gain or profit. The use of short quotations or occasional page copying for personal or group study is permitted and encouraged. Permission will be granted upon request. Unless otherwise identified, Scripture quotations are from the King James Version of the Bible.

Take note that the name satan and related names are not capitalized. We choose not to acknowledge him, even to the point of violating grammatical rules.

Treasure House
An Imprint of
Destiny Image
P.O. Box 310
Shippensburg, PA 17257

"For where your treasure is
there will your heart be also." Matthew 6:21

ISBN 1-56043-782-0

For Worldwide Distribution
Printed in the U.S.A.

Destiny Image books are available through these fine distributors outside the United States:

Christian Growth, Inc.	Successful Christian Living
Jalan Kilang-Timor, Singapore 0315	Capetown, Rep. of South Africa
Lifestream	Vision Resources
Nottingham, England	Ponsonby, Auckland, New Zealand
Rhema Ministries Trading	WA Buchanan Company
Randburg, South Africa	Geebung, Queensland, Austrailia
Salvation Book Centre	Word Alive
Pelgaling, Jaya, Malaysia	Niverville, Manitoba, Canada

Contents

Chapter		Page
	Preface	v
1	A Church of Power Is Emerging	1
2	Who Will Get the Power?	41
3	The Foundation of the Church	83
4	The Fivefold Ministry	107
5	The Apostle	119
6	The Prophet	151
7	The Evangelist	173
8	The Pastor	185
9	Church Government	195
	Conclusion	213
	Epilogue	215

Preface

Serious times are ahead for the world in which we live. Technology has advanced at an accelerated rate in this past century, not always to our advantage; we approach the year 2000 with a potential for the total annihilation of the people on this planet. Nuclear war, biological experimentation, environmental hazards, the hole in the ozone layer, the plague of AIDS all are a threat to mankind. What will be next? How long will man survive the quickening pace of his quest for advancement?

Adding to the turmoil on this planet earth, wars and rumors of war have not waned but intensified. Just in the past 50 years the world has suffered through two world wars. Instead of peace, there is ever-present hostility and unrest.

Yet, while all this unfolds before our eyes, we in America have more time available to indulge in the pleasures of this world. Our moral values have deteriorated to the point that man is more in love with the ways of the world than the ways of God.

All this should cause the Christian to ask himself, "What impact is the Church having on the world today?"

The Church has been in a dark age for centuries. Only in the past several hundred years have we seen the Word of God opened up to all Christians. More recently many Christians have experienced the baptism in the Holy Spirit, as described in the Book of Acts, and begun again to believe in a supernatural God who desires to manifest Himself in the working of miracles and signs and wonders.

I believe, brothers and sisters, we are at the brink of an era in which the Church will experience a tremendous spiritual breakthrough. Quick and mighty advancements will be made by our Lord in the building of His Church before He returns. Now is the time for the Christian to get serious. There is little time to waste. The Church will return to the scriptural ways that we see in the Book of Acts. When the Lord returns for His bride she will be a glorious Church, one that has been mightily confronting the devil for the souls of mankind. She will be a Church endued with Holy Spirit power as never before seen, that will powerfully affect the world.

This is an intense and serious book for the Christian who is hungry and thirsting and who wants to be a part of God's next great move. It is for the Christian who values God's ways above man's. God is doing a new thing. Don't miss it!

1

A Church of Power Is Emerging

A Prophetic Word

In the late 1980's, I attended a weekly citywide prayer meeting. At one of the meetings there was a word from the Lord that the meetings were to cease. As leader, I was faced with a difficult decision, but I knew this word was from the Lord and that I needed to obey. I went home with my head bowed, wondering what the Lord was up to.

For days and months I sought the Lord. A theme concerning power surfaced that caused me to diligently study the Scriptures. The Lord revealed much to me concerning His Church, and it seemed as though He would have me to write a book. One morning in prayer I asked the Lord what I was to title this book. Without directly answering my question He spoke in a very powerful way and said, *"A Church of power is emerging."*

Having focused on this topic for months, I clearly understood what the Lord meant. Soon, very soon, a great move of God will occur. We will see the Church endued with power as never before. Pentecostal power is what I am referring to. The same Holy Spirit who visited the Body of Christ in the upper room on Pentecost will visit local bodies again, and the Holy Spirit fire will fall.

I am convinced that the established Church today is missing the manifestation of the power of God as we so magnificently see it in the Book of Acts. Where are the miracles, signs and wonders? Something is wrong with the existing Church. Countless Christians who frequent churches of all denominations easily support this observation. The Spirit within them witnesses that something is missing. Beloved, I say to you very confidently: *A Church of power is emerging.*

A Manifestation of Power

As we look at the life of Jesus in the four gospels, we find countless examples of Jesus healing people, delivering them from demons and performing miracles, signs and wonders. We see a manifestation of power in the walk of Christ. *To manifest* means "to show openly; to publicly demonstrate." Jesus publicly demonstrated the power of the Holy Spirit throughout His ministry on earth.

This same manifestation of power continued in the life of the apostles and other disciples of the Lord. The Book of Acts is filled with demonstrations of the power of the Holy Spirit. On Pentecost, Peter preached an anointed message. Shortly thereafter Peter healed a crippled man. The Bible says, "And by the hands of the apostles were many signs and wonders wrought among the people..." (Acts 5:12). We also see that the disciple Philip went down to a city in Samaria to proclaim Christ there, and everyone paid close attention to the miraculous signs he did. Then there was the apostle Paul who came preaching "...not with enticing words of man's wisdom, but in demonstration of the Spirit and of power..." (1 Cor. 2:4).

But what about today? Where is the demonstration of the Spirit and power? With the ascension of Christ, the death of the 12 apostles and the early saints, and the close of the New Testament Scriptures, has the manifestation of the power of God ceased?

A Church of Power Is Emerging

We don't see many healings and miracles today. Many pastors readily admit they do not see or experience the power of God. Therefore, some have come to the natural conclusion that these things have passed away, that there had been a dispensation of miracles and signs. Of what little of the miraculous we do see, some has been exaggerated. I say this based on the Scriptures. If we return to the example of Peter healing the man crippled from birth, we read in Acts 3:6-8,

> *Then Peter said, Silver and gold have I none; but such as I have give I thee: In the name of Jesus Christ of Nazareth rise up and walk. And he took him by the right hand, and lifted him up: and immediately his feet and ankle bones received strength. And he leaping up stood, and walked, and entered with them into the temple, walking, and leaping, and praising God.*

Instantly the power of God made this man whole. It did not take a long-winded prayer. The man's reaction of leaping and praising God is what you might expect of someone who had been impaired from birth and in one brief moment made well. But go to a service where spiritual healing is practiced, and very seldom will you see this happen. You might see a man or woman called forth, prayed for and prayed for, but nothing happens. That person is then told that he or she is healed and to claim the healing and start praising God, believing that they are well. Yet the expression and the reaction of the individual who had been prayed for would not indicate a miracle. Often, intimidated by the speaker and the crowd, this person will pretend that he or she is healed to be spared the embarrassment of his or her lack of faith.

Saints, you can name it, you can claim it, you can praise God or say whatever you want, but the fact remains that when you are prayed for, either the power of God touches you or it doesn't.

I believe that this failure transpires in our Christian circles for lack of spiritual teaching and guidance, but mostly because the true power of God is missing. Many Christians believe in healing and miracles but have never been properly discipled. Still the fact remains that the power of God is missing in the Body of Christ.

In wondering what the world will be like just before the Lord comes, the following is an interesting passage of Scripture:

This know also, that in the last days perilous times shall come. For men shall be lovers of their own selves, covetous, boasters, proud, blasphemers, disobedient to parents, unthankful, unholy, without natural affection, trucebreakers, false accusers, incontinent, fierce, despisers of those that are good, traitors, heady, highminded, lovers of pleasures more than lovers of God; having a form of godliness, but denying the power thereof: from such turn away. 2 Timothy 3:1-5

Verse 4 seems to indicate that churchgoing people will dabble with the world and dabble with God, but they will be *more* in love with the pleasures of the world than with God. In the United States never before have we had not only more time but also more money to indulge in pleasure seeking. Television, videos, computer games, movies, sporting events, luxurious restaurants, resorts and spas, partying and revelry dominate our life style. Yet, the same people who indulge in these diversions attend church on Sunday, thinking they can appease God in this way. As it says in verse 5, they have a form of godliness.

I also find it interesting that the very last evil mentioned is that those pretending to have a form of godliness—those pretending to be the true Church—will actually deny the power of God. This is exactly what is being perpetrated in the Church today. Many Christians don't believe in the Pentecostal power. They trust more in what they see than in what the Word of God says. Other Christians are taught by their pastors and leaders that the Pentecostal power has been dispensed with. Pastors misinterpret and wrongly teach according to what they experience in their own lives. This supernatural power with which God intended all believers to be clothed is ignored and actually denied by the Church today. What a strategic plan of satan. I'm glad I serve a God who has a greater plan.

The following passage of Scripture reveals a little of God's nature and plan.

And as Jesus passed by, He saw a man which was blind from his birth. And His disciples asked Him, saying, Master, who did sin, this man, or his parents, that he was born blind? Jesus answered, Neither hath this man sinned, nor his parents: but that the works of God should be made manifest in him. I must work the works of Him that sent Me, while it is day: the night cometh, when no man can work. As long as I am in the world, I am the light of the world. When He had thus spoken, He spat on the ground, and made clay of the spittle, and He anointed the eyes of the blind man with the clay, and said unto him, Go, wash in the pool of Siloam, (which is by interpretation, Sent). He went his way therefore, and washed, and came seeing. John 9:1-7

We see the disciples somewhat confused over the issue at hand. This incident occurred that "the works of God should be made manifest." The healing of this blind man was not so much the work of

A Church of Power Is Emerging

Jesus as it was the work of God the Father. It was the work of the one who had sent Him. It illustrates not so much the work of one man, Jesus, as much as the nature of the God we serve. God's nature is to do good, to make man whole. Our God has a nature that delights in seeing His children healed and made well. Since God does not change, His nature and will being the same, we should believe that the same miraculous power that Jesus displayed and that we see in the life of the early Church still holds true today. God intends that His works should be made manifest. God intends that everyone in the Body of Christ experience a manifestation of power in their lives. God intends that *you* experience a manifestation of power in your life.

Let us be honest with ourselves. Except in a few cases, the Holy Spirit power is missing. It's missing in our lives and in the life of the Church. Enough pretending; we need Him, the Holy Spirit. We need the anointing to preach, and we need the power to heal the sick, to cast out demons and to do miracles, signs and wonders. We need the real stuff.

In the last days, amidst countless numbers in the churches who have fallen in love with the pleasures of life—sexual immorality and promiscuity and pornography; fallen in love with television, video games and movies; fallen in love with football, baseball, golfing, bowling, fishing and the like; fallen in love with

A Church of Power Is Emerging

going out to eat and to shop for expensive things and with dancing and social gatherings; amidst countless churches who have an outward appearance of being godly but inside are filled with greedy, lustful, unholy people; amidst countless churches who deny the power of God; amidst these I declare that *a Church of power is emerging.*

The Church Is in Error

There is a wide spectrum of Christians today with all sorts of doctrines, beliefs and practices. From laymen to pastors, from Roman Catholic to the latest Pentecostal churches, there are varying views of the Pentecostal power of healing and miracles. Most are disbelievers. Jesus was faced with a similar circumstance in Matthew 22:23-33.

> *The same day came to Him the Sadducees, which say that there is no resurrection, and asked Him, saying, Master, Moses said, If a man die, having no children, his brother shall marry his wife, and raise up seed unto his brother. Now there were with us seven brethren: and the first, when he had married a wife, deceased, and having no issue, left his wife unto his brother: Likewise the second also, and the third, unto the seventh. And last of all the woman died also. Therefore in the resurrection whose wife*

shall she be of the seven? for they all had her. Jesus answered and said unto them, Ye do err, not knowing the scriptures, nor the power of God. For in the resurrection they neither marry, nor are given in marriage, but are as the angels of God in heaven. But as touching the resurrection of the dead, have ye not read that which was spoken unto you by God, saying, I am the God of Abraham, and the God of Isaac, and the God of Jacob? God is not the God of the dead, but of the living. And when the multitude heard this, they were astonished at His doctrine.

There were those who approached Jesus who did not believe in the resurrection of the dead. Jesus' response to them, basically, was that they were in error. They were in error because they did not know the Scriptures nor the power of God. Likewise, the Church today is in error because we do not know the Scriptures nor the power of God.

Jesus would simply say to us, "Have you not read the Scriptures?"

For John truly baptized with water; but ye shall be baptized with the Holy Ghost not many days hence.... But ye shall receive power, after that the Holy Ghost is come upon you: and ye shall be witnesses unto Me both in Jerusalem, and in all

Judaea, and in Samaria, and unto the uttermost part of the earth. Acts 1:5,8

We do err. We are in error because we do not know the Scriptures, and we are in error because we do not know the power of God.

To err, according to *Vine's Expository Dictionary* means "to cause to wander, lead astray, deceive." That is exactly what the devil has done to the Church over the past 2,000 years; he has deceived us and talked us out of the divine, miraculous power of the Holy Spirit that we see everywhere in the Book of Acts. How sad.

To err also means "to miss the mark; to fail." That is exactly the same definition as of the Greek word *hamartia*, "to sin." So, to err or to miss the mark is to sin. Let me put it this way: to go forth and preach the gospel without the anointing of the Holy Spirit, to not see signs following the preaching of the gospel, is to *err*, to miss the mark, to fail. Therefore, the Church is in sin because it does not know the power of God. This may be difficult for you to hear, but our God desires His Church to be all that He has declared it to be.

Jesus said, "God is not the God of the dead, but of the living."

Our God is not a God of mechanical wizardry, but a God who is "the Anointed One."

Our God is not a God of sickness and disease. He is a God who heals.

Our God is not a God with a short arm, who has dispensed with miracles, signs and wonders. He is a God who stretches out His arm to perform mighty miracles and wonders.

Our God is not a God who denies us power, but a God who released His power on Pentecost.

If you do not see the power of God, something is wrong. You're in error. You're in sin.

Concerning Jesus, the Scripture says, "And declared to be the Son of God with power, according to the spirit of holiness, by the resurrection from the dead..." (Rom. 1:4). Likewise, I believe that soon a remnant Church will be resurrected, will emerge and be declared with *power*.

The Purpose for the Holy Spirit Power

Forty days after the ascension of Jesus Christ His followers were gathered together in the upper room, and the Holy Spirit came down from Heaven and rested upon each of them. They all were filled with the Holy Spirit and began to speak in other tongues. Those who heard thought these people were drunk, but the apostle Peter stood up and explained that this was what had been foretold by the prophet Joel, that in the last days God would pour out His Spirit upon all flesh and that sons and daughters would prophesy, young men would see visions, etc.

Peter continued to preach that this Jesus whom they had crucified was both Lord and Christ and that they should repent in the name of Jesus for the forgiveness of their sins. Those who accepted this message were about 3,000. This is the account of Pentecost as recorded in the second chapter of the Book of Acts. Not a bad day for the Kingdom of God!

What actually happened on Pentecost? Jesus simply stated to the disciples that they should wait for the Holy Spirit to come and that the Holy Spirit would come upon them and they would receive power (Acts 1:4-8). Speaking in tongues was a manifestation of the Holy Spirit in power. Just think, Jesus Himself had trained the disciples for three years, He had given them specific orders before His departure, and then His one last command was to *wait*, to wait for the Holy Spirit to come upon them. In Luke 24:49, Jesus said, "And, behold, I send the promise of My Father upon you: but tarry ye in the city of Jerusalem, until ye be endued with power from on high." The disciples would be *endued* with power. *Endued* means "to provide with ability."

Think about this for a moment. Despite the teachings of Jesus, despite all the lessons and despite all the on-the-job training, they still lacked the ability.

They lacked an important ingredient, a supernatural empowerment—the Holy Spirit. The disciples rightfully waited, and what a difference it made! We now have the Book of Acts. If they hadn't waited, there would be no Book of Acts!

There are thousands upon thousands of Christians supposedly ministering in the name of the Lord who do not have this ability that only the Holy Spirit can provide. These Christians, many of them leaders in the Church, have all sorts of degrees and education, yet they are missing the power. The Church needs to see more days like Pentecost, more preachers like Peter.

Why don't we see this power? Why don't we see a manifestation of the Holy Spirit in the life of Christians? Because our purpose for the power is not God's purpose.

Our God is a God of purpose. There is a purpose for the creation of mankind. God has a purpose for you. God has a purpose for the Church. God had a purpose for sending the Holy Spirit on Pentecost.

Webster's Dictionary defines *purpose* as "a result which it is desired to obtain and which is kept in mind in performing an action." God has a desired result every time the Holy Spirit power becomes manifest. We're talking about a manifestation of an awesome, indescribable, unequaled, supernatural power.

A Church of Power Is Emerging

You would not think of giving an eight-year-old child a hundred dollar bill to go down to the end of the street to buy whatever he pleased. You would be looking at a bag filled with candy, ice cream and other assorted junk. I don't believe that God casually hands out His Holy Spirit power to infants. God has a purpose for this baptism in the Holy Spirit. That purpose is very focused, which we shall soon see. It would behoove us to study the Word of God to find out the purpose for this Holy Spirit power that is available to all Christians.

To make this all a little clearer, let's return to our definition of purpose. This was the definition of *purpose*: "a result which it is desired to obtain and which is kept in mind in performing an action." Slightly rearranged this reads as follows: to perform an action to obtain a desired result. Now, let's break up this definition into parts.

To perform	*an action*	*to obtain*	*a desired*	*result*
to do	preaching	to possess	motives	souls saved
to go	witnessing	to take back from the devil	to please God	salvation
to confront	healing			
to act	deliverance			
	miracles			
	signs			
	wonders			

We already know that the Holy Spirit is to give us power to enable us. Yet, God had a special purpose in mind for sending the Holy Spirit on Pentecost. As we look at the chart, it can help us to see the whole of God's purpose.

We see five parts to God's purpose: *to perform–an action–to obtain–desired–result*. First, let's consider *action*. In general, the Holy Spirit comes upon us to endue us, to give us ability to take action, thus we have the Book of Acts. What kind of action? I believe the best way to study this would be to look at the life of Jesus and then the lives of the disciples whom Jesus trained. Remember, our actions need to be scriptural. The Bible is our guide.

Let's begin with the life of Jesus.

Jesus was baptized in the Jordan River by John the Baptist; the Holy Spirit came upon Him as He was baptized. Jesus was then led by the Holy Spirit into the wilderness where He was tempted by satan for 40 days. He then returned to Galilee "in the power of the Spirit." Shortly thereafter Jesus entered the synagogue in Nazareth, stood up and read a passage from the Book of Isaiah:

> *The Spirit of the Lord is upon Me, because He hath anointed Me to preach the gospel to the poor; He hath sent Me to heal the brokenhearted, to preach deliverance to the captives, and recovering of sight to the blind, to set at liberty them that are bruised, to preach the acceptable year of the Lord.* Luke 4:18-19

Jesus went on to say unto them, "This day is this scripture fulfilled in your ears" (Lk. 4:21), meaning this Scripture referred to Himself.

From the very beginning of His ministry, Jesus knew the purpose for which He had been anointed by the Holy Spirit. This passage could not be any more clear. Jesus was anointed to preach. Preaching is mentioned three times in the above Scripture. Jesus also was anointed, baptized in the Holy Spirit, for healing, deliverance and working of miracles. We need only to continue to the end of the fourth chapter of Luke to see what Jesus' ministry was all about:

Deliverance—"...for with authority and power He commandeth the unclean spirits, and they come out" (v. 36).

Healing—"...all they that had any sick with divers diseases brought them unto Him; and He laid His hands on every one of them, and healed them" (v. 40).

Preaching—"...I must preach the kingdom of God to other cities also: for therefore am I sent. And He preached in the synagogues of Galilee" (vv. 43-44).

Jesus also did many miracles, signs and wonders. "And many other signs truly did Jesus in the presence of His disciples, which are not written in this book" (Jn. 20:30).

Jesus' three years of ministry were ones of confrontation, of action. The purpose for the Holy Spirit, for power coming upon the Lord, was to preach, to heal, to deliver men from demons and to do signs and wonders and miracles.

Now to completely understand the purpose for the Holy Spirit coming upon our Lord, we need to know *the desired result*. The Bible says Jesus was sent "to seek and to save that which was lost" (Lk. 19:10), "to save sinners" (1 Tim. 1:15). It was for salvation that Jesus came.

To summarize, Jesus was anointed by the Holy Spirit to preach, to heal the sick, to cast out demons, to do signs, wonders and miracles so that sinners would be saved.

Now, what about the 12 disciples? How close will their ministry parallel that of Jesus Christ?

Here is a command that Jesus gave to the Twelve during their training:

These twelve Jesus sent forth, and commanded them, saying, Go not into the way of the Gentiles, and into any city of the Samaritans enter ye not: But go rather to the lost sheep of the house of Israel.

A Church of Power Is Emerging

And as ye go, preach, saying, The kingdom of heaven is at hand. Heal the sick, cleanse the lepers, raise the dead, cast out devils: freely ye have received, freely give. Matthew 10:5-8

They, too, were to go to the lost. They, too, were to preach, to heal the sick, to do miracles and to cast out demons. From the moment Jesus asked them to follow Him, they were told the purpose: to become fishers of men (Mt. 4:19). Many others, I believe, wanted to follow the Lord. Jesus told one man who wanted first to go bury his father, "Let the dead bury their dead: but go thou and preach the kingdom of God" (Lk. 9:60). We see Jesus sending out 70 other disciples, in the beginning of the tenth chapter of Luke with similar instructions. He began His instructions with the comment, "The harvest truly is great, but the labourers are few: pray ye therefore the Lord of the harvest, that He would send forth labourers into His harvest."

With the population of the world growing by leaps and bounds from approximately 5 billion in 1990 to an estimated 6.5 billion by the year 2000, there will be a brand new harvest field of 1.5 billion people. Even in America, which in most Third World countries is thought to be a Christian nation, we know that churches are growing cold, that the gospel is not being preached and that the generations to come will be lost unless something changes.

The harvest truly is great. But where are the laborers? Where are the Christians who would gladly go out to proclaim the gospel? I'll tell you. Some are pursuing their own gain. They are pursuing material things and worldly wealth. Still others in the Church want to be involved in ministries with which they feel comfortable. Singing in the church choir is very comfortable. Simply taking the youth out for a picnic or sporting event is comfortable. Cooking, serving and attending church banquets and luncheons is comfortable.

I could go on and on with a list of activities that are comfortable. The shame of it all is most Christians believe these are the areas of service to which God has called them in the Church. And in most local churches these are the only activities in which one can participate. Pastors encourage their flock to be involved in them. But beloved, Jesus never intended you to be rich, famous or comfortable on this planet. Jesus intended you to go out into the harvest field, no matter what the cost.

The tremendous importance of preaching, healing the sick, casting out demons, of miracles, signs and wonders can be seen when we come to the end of each of the gospels. Jesus gave the disciples a final command:

> *And He said unto them, Go ye into all the world, and preach the gospel to every creature. He that believeth and is baptized shall be saved; but he that believeth not shall be damned. And these signs shall follow them that believe; in My name shall they cast out devils; they shall speak with new tongues; they shall take up serpents; and if they drink any deadly thing, it shall not hurt them; they shall lay hands on the sick, and they shall recover.* Mark 16:15-18

I believe that Jesus was very serious when He gave the disciples this order. He focused the disciples' thoughts on the severity of the gospel message. Those who do not believe in the gospel message are damned. They are condemned to spend eternity in hell. But those who do believe will be saved.

Jesus also said this to His disciples prior to leaving them, "Peace be unto you: as My Father hath sent Me, even so send I you" (Jn. 20:21). As Jesus was sent, so would the disciples be sent. As Jesus was sent to preach, so were the disciples. As Jesus was sent to heal the sick, so were the disciples. As Jesus was sent to confront the enemy and to cast out demons, so were the disciples. As Jesus was sent to seek and to save the lost, so were the disciples.

A Church of Power Is Emerging

And likewise, as Jesus was sent under the anointing of the Holy Spirit, so too were the disciples sent out under the power of the Holy Spirit.

As you read the Book of Acts, you will see that the gospel spread rapidly throughout the world because the early disciples carried out their marching orders under the power of the Holy Spirit. They preached; they healed the sick; they cast out demons; and they performed miracles and signs and wonders.

Yes, these are the *actions* of a disciple. But mere knowledge of this fact is not enough. Another part of our chart is *to perform*. We are *to do*, we are *to go*, we are *to confront*. We have many Christians in many churches doing many things, and yet they never experience the Holy Spirit coming upon them in power. Then they say, "Why don't we see a manifestation of the Holy Spirit?" Why? Because they don't *do* the *RIGHT* action. God is always looking for an available Christian *to send*.

Beloved, the Church is merrily going down the path of least resistance, of no conflict, of complacency. We stay in the confines of the four walls of the church and hold our Bible classes, our seminars, our musical concerts, our breakfasts and dinners. Some pastors teach the right things, but live a hypocritical life. They never do the very things they proclaim. The devil is laughing at us. The devil probably mocks the Church in the face of the Lord. "Look at these so-called Christians," the devil says, "all they do is talk. They're nothing but talk."

Brothers and sisters, my Bible tells me, "...the kingdom of heaven suffereth violence, and the violent take it by force" (Mt. 11:12). Jesus is looking for "violent" Christians, for a "violent" Church, for a people who will take action, for a people who will go and preach the gospel and heal the sick.

As our chart points out, while we perform our actions they are *to obtain* a desired result. Jesus didn't come down to earth to do a lot of amazing things to impress us. He didn't use the Holy Spirit power to dazzle the Jewish leaders. Jesus knew there was a battle going on. We need to know that we are at war. The enemy is the devil and every one of his demonic followers.

The devil has blinded the minds of unbelievers so they cannot see the light of the gospel (see 2 Cor. 4:4). Jesus came to destroy the devil's work (1 John 3:8). Jesus knew He was at war with the devil, that the devil had a grip on mankind, that He had come to set the captives free and that they would be saved. Every deed that Jesus performed, every individual healed, every demon rebuked, every miracle and sign and wonder was to overcome the work of the devil. Disciples of the Lord need to keep this in mind: we are at war, we have a distinct enemy—the devil and his wicked horde of demons—and we fight for souls. Christian, you're not saved to play golf, baseball, football or basketball; you're not saved to play video games or sit in front of the TV set. You've been saved to join the army of the Lord and to win souls.

Let's "get real." The devil controls our schools, our places of work, our institutions, our government and the non-Christian family; he controls our streets and our parks and our cities. The Holy Spirit power is for taking back from satan that which belongs to God, it is for possessing our cities and our land, it is for the souls of mankind.

There is one last point in our definition of purpose that we need to discuss, that is *desire*. Winning souls is a *desired* result when the Holy Spirit comes upon us to preach. You see, the reason we are saved is not merely because we were created by God, the devil has taken us away from the Creator, and God the Almighty wants to get us back. Heaven forbid! No! Believe me when I say this, God *greatly* desires that we be saved. God's love for us is beyond your understanding or mine. He greatly desires that none be lost.

Recall the story of the prodigal son from the 15th chapter of Luke. This is how the father greeted the son when he returned:

A Church of Power Is Emerging

But when he was yet a great way off, his father saw him, and had compassion, and ran, and fell on his neck, and kissed him. And the son said unto him, Father, I have sinned against heaven, and in thy sight, and am no more worthy to be called thy son. But the father said to his servants, Bring forth the best robe, and put it on him; and put a ring on his hand, and shoes on his feet: and bring hither the fatted calf, and kill it; and let us eat, and be merry: for this my son was dead, and is alive again; he was lost, and is found. And they began to be merry. Luke 15:20-24

This is an example of how happy our heavenly Father is when but one lost soul is saved. Jesus also had a great desire to win the lost. Jesus loved them and had compassion for them because they were like lost sheep. I believe that this attitude of love and compassion was passed on to the disciples as they watched the Lord minister. We need to examine our hearts. Do we really desire to see souls saved or do we just talk?

Brothers and sisters in the Lord, there is not some fancy formula for getting the Holy Spirit power. The chart based on the definition of purpose is to give us a broader picture of God. Yes, God is sovereign and can do whatever He pleases, but He also has a plan and purpose for everything He does. There is more to receiving the power of the Holy Spirit than acts of

A Church of Power Is Emerging

power, miracles and preaching a witty homily; we need to keep in mind that the Holy Spirit power was given to confront the enemy for lost souls.

There is an example from the Word of God that summarizes all that we have talked about in this section. In the fourth chapter of the Book of Acts the Holy Spirit was poured again on the believers. Peter and John were going to the temple to pray when they met a beggar crippled from birth. Peter prayed for the man and he was healed. This afforded Peter the opportunity to preach the gospel again, whereby the number of men who believed grew to about 5,000. At the same time, the priests and the captain of the temple guard and the Sadducees (who did not believe in the resurrection) were greatly disturbed and arrested Peter and John because they were teaching the people and proclaiming in Jesus the resurrection of the dead. The next day Peter and John were brought before the elders and teachers of the law, questioned, commanded not to speak or teach at all in the name of Jesus and then let go. Peter and John returned to their people and reported all that was said unto them. The Bible says,

> *...they lifted up their voice to God with one accord, and said, Lord, Thou art God, which hast made heaven, and earth, and the sea, and all that in them is: Who by the mouth of Thy servant David hast said, Why did the heathen rage, and*

the people imagine vain things? The kings of the earth stood up, and the rulers were gathered together against the Lord, and against His Christ. For a truth against Thy holy child Jesus, whom Thou hast anointed, both Herod, and Pontius Pilate, with the Gentiles, and the people of Israel, were gathered together, for to do whatsoever Thy hand and Thy counsel determined before to be done. And now, Lord, behold their threatenings: and grant unto Thy servants, that with all boldness they may speak Thy word, by stretching forth Thine hand to heal; and that signs and wonders may be done by the name of Thy holy child Jesus.

And when they had prayed, the place was shaken where they were assembled together; and they were all filled with the Holy Ghost, and they spake the word of God with boldness. Acts 4:24-31

There is much we can learn from just a few verses of Scripture. Notice how short a prayer this was, yet the Holy Spirit fell and filled all the people just as on Pentecost. Why? Because they prayed, as Jesus had trained them, to speak the Word and to heal the sick. They also prayed for *great* boldness to *do* these things, knowing they risked being persecuted for the name of Jesus. They all were in one accord; they all agreed and knew this was what they needed the

Holy Spirit power for. The Holy Spirit shook the place and filled them because what they had prayed for lined up with God's scriptural purpose for sending the Holy Spirit.

What happened as this group of Christians prayed was they received the "real stuff," a genuine pouring out of the Holy Spirit. We need the "real stuff"!

Church, you can pray for hours on end, you can hold your prayer meetings once a week, daily or all night if you wish, but you will never experience a genuine Pentecostal outpouring of the Holy Spirit until you have God's purpose in mind.

They Spake the Word of God

We finished the previous section with the passage of Scripture from Acts 4 which ended this way: "...and they were all filled with the Holy Ghost, and they spake the word of God with boldness" (v. 31).

Having prayed for the ability to speak the Word, to heal and to do signs and wonders, it is recorded only that they spoke the Word of God. If we were to continue reading in Acts, we surely would see many healings and signs and wonders, but it becomes obvious from the above Scripture that what was of primary importance was *to speak the Word*. Consider these Scriptures from the Book of Acts:

A Church of Power Is Emerging

And the word of God increased.... Acts 6:7

But the word of God grew and multiplied. Acts 12:24

And the word of the Lord was published throughout all the region. Acts 13:49

So mightily grew the word of God and prevailed. Acts 19:20

It was the Word of God, the Word of the Lord that was spreading throughout the land. What was "the Word"? The Word was "of the Lord," meaning all that Jesus said and did. It was the gospel, the good news of salvation through Jesus Christ. It was the remission of sins by His death on the cross. It was eternal life by the resurrection of Jesus from the grave.

Consider again this familiar passage:

For whosoever shall call upon the name of the Lord shall be saved. How then shall they call on Him in whom they have not believed? and how shall they believe in Him of whom they have not heard? and how shall they hear without a preacher? And how shall they preach, except they be sent? as it is written, How beautiful are the feet of them that preach the gospel of

peace, and bring glad tidings of good things!
Romans 10:13-15

Here we have a progression: *being sent–preaching (the gospel)–hearing–believing–calling on the name of the Lord–salvation.*

This is how people are saved. They must hear the gospel preached. The Word of the Lord must be spoken. Something happens when we preach the gospel, something supernatural. Following are two more passages that will help us to see the dynamics of the spoken Word:

And take the helmet of salvation, and the sword of the Spirit, which is the word of God.... Ephesians 6:17

For the word of God is quick, and powerful, and sharper than any two-edged sword, piercing even to the dividing asunder of soul and spirit, and of the joints and marrow, and is a discerner of the thoughts and intents of the heart. Hebrews 4:12

The Word of God acts as a sword of the Spirit. It is powerful. It is sharp and piercing and acts quickly. Think of someone sticking a sword into you, this is what it is like. This sword pierces your thoughts and the intents of your heart. The most personal, intimate, vulnerable part of you is pierced by Someone else, the Holy Spirit.

Think of a lost, degenerate, disgusting soul steeped in sexual perversion, longing every moment of the day to fulfill the sexual appetite without regard to consequence. The fleshly pleasure of this sexual experience outweighs any thoughts of giving it up. Over and over again acts of perversion are committed in the face of the Creator, because the ruler of this world, the devil, has blinded the mind from perceiving the truth—a sad state for man or woman to be in. It is only the Word of God that can pierce through the demonic hold on this person. It's powerful, it's quick. It bears the truth to the heart and mind and soul, coming against every lie that satan has established, especially the truth regarding Jesus Christ as the way to salvation.

Jesus said to His disciples that it was expedient that He go away, then He would send the Comforter, the Holy Spirit.

And when He is come, He will reprove the world of sin, and of righteousness, and of judgment: of sin, because they believe not on Me; of righteousness, because I go to My Father, and ye see Me no more; of judgment, because the prince of this world is judged. John 16:8-11

Reprove here means "to convict." The Holy Spirit in this passage is again acting as a sword to convict the lost souls concerning sin, concerning righteousness and concerning judgment.

Oh, Church! If only we would see "how beautiful are the feet of them that preach the gospel of peace." The Word of God must go forth under the power of the Holy Spirit.

Recalling the previous section, we saw that the purpose of the baptism of the Holy Spirit was to give us ability to "perform an action to obtain a desired result" and that the scriptural actions are to preach, to heal, to cast out demons and to perform signs and wonders. Now, we see the importance of preaching the Word, the Holy Spirit is at work bringing conviction, which leads to repentance and salvation. But what then is the importance of healing, deliverance and miracles? We shall see.

And He said unto them, Go ye into all the world, and preach the gospel to every creature. He that believeth and is baptized shall be saved; but he that believeth not shall be damned. And these signs shall follow them that believe; In My name shall they cast out devils; they shall speak with new tongues; they shall take up serpents; and if they drink any deadly thing, it shall not hurt them; they shall lay hands on the sick, and they shall recover. So then after the Lord had spoken unto them, He was received up into heaven, and sat on the right hand of God. And they went forth, and preached every where, the Lord working with them, and confirming the word with signs following. Amen. Mark 16:15-20

A Church of Power Is Emerging

Here is a revealing Scripture regarding the relationship between preaching the Word and healing, casting out demons and miracles. The Scripture says that the *Word* was *confirmed* by the signs that followed. There is no doubt left as to the place of preaching the gospel and healing and working of miracles. Of first importance is preaching. In Luke 4:18, Jesus was anointed first to preach. Signs, then, are secondary, to confirm the Word. Yes, they are important, but only in respect to the Word. This is a very significant point.

Following is an example in the life of Paul and Barnabas:

At Iconium Paul and Barnabas went as usual into the Jewish synagogue. There they spoke so effectively that a great number of Jews and Gentiles believed. But the Jews who refused to believe stirred up the Gentiles and poisoned their minds against the brothers. So Paul and Barnabas spent considerable time there, speaking boldly for the Lord, who confirmed the message of His grace by enabling them to do miraculous signs and wonders. Acts 14:1-3, NIV

We see that many believed because of the Word of the gospel being preached, and the Lord confirmed this message by enabling Paul and Barnabas to do signs and wonders. Miracles made people take notice of the words that were being proclaimed. They added tremendous weight to the gospel. It is very likely that these people had never before seen people cured of diseases or healed of sickness. No doubt they were struck with awe and believed the words of these men. In these last days we surely need the power of God so that the Christian can be set apart from the world, set apart from the doctors with their scalpels and prescriptions. Jesus never used a scalpel or prescribed a medicine. Jesus spoke the Word and they were healed.

The world needs to see the Christian as one whom "God is with," as it was in the days of Moses. It needs to be the message of the Christian, the gospel message, that the world pays attention to. Yes, miracles, signs and wonders can have a tremendous effect. But, it is the gospel through which people hear and are saved.

When the paralytic was lowered through the roof of the house where Jesus was preaching, Jesus first said to him, "Son, thy sins be forgiven thee" (Mk. 2:5). To confirm His word He then healed the paralytic. With Jesus, getting right with God took precedence over getting healed. Having sins forgiven was of greater value than being healed. Jesus knew His mission on earth was not to rid man of all sickness and disease, but to save man, to reconcile man to God.

A Church of Power Is Emerging

The Church today, however, has been mesmerized by those with "healing ministries." People flock to healing seminars, to large stadiums where healing exhibitions are put on. There are Christians who judge the outcome by how good the music is and how many people are slain in the spirit. Some churches now have turned from preaching the Word to *specializing* in the healing ministry. Schools specialize in healing, and some Christians specialize in healing. Some of the reasons for this can be seen in the Word of God.

"And a great multitude followed Him, because they saw His miracles which He did on them that were diseased" (Jn. 6:2). There were throngs of people who followed Jesus everywhere He went because of the miracles He performed. Healing and miracles attract people. There are Christians ministering today who are taking the quick road to stardom and fame. They want to get ahead and know the quickest way is to get a large following. They believe a ministry of healing and miracles is the way to go. Not only can it be glamorous, but extremely profitable. Churches have even taken names that focus on healing or deliverance or miracles.

"Then those men, when they had seen the miracle that Jesus did, said, This is of a truth that prophet that should come into the world" (Jn. 6:14). Many who followed Jesus believed He was not a common man, but more—a prophet, because of His miracles. Christians are consumed with prophetic ministry more than anything in these last days. Performing a miracle gives some sort of credence to one's identity as a prophet. Doing strange "prophetic" things that come true makes one out to be a prophet. In somehow making the people believe that a person has been healed, when in fact he has not, people will say one is a prophet. Believe me when I say that there are those Christians consumed with this kind of thinking. They will go to any length to get a large crowd or have people call them prophet.

It appears the Body of Christ has lost all sense of direction and purpose. The world has crept into the Church: bigness, showmanship, glamor, power and wealth have overwhelmed the Christian's thinking. Where is the gospel preached? Not on the streets. Not house to house. Not in the house of God. How many faithful Christians are there in the local body who obey and go forth proclaiming the good news? Our thoughts should be on preaching the gospel, on getting souls saved, on making disciples.

There is another reason for the manifestation of the Holy Spirit in healing, signs and wonders. The apostle Paul proclaimed these words:

And I, brethren, when I came to you, came not with excellency of speech or of wisdom, declaring

A Church of Power Is Emerging

unto you the testimony of God. For I determined not to know any thing among you, save Jesus Christ, and Him crucified. And I was with you in weakness, and in fear, and in much trembling. And my speech and my preaching was not with enticing words of man's wisdom, but in demonstration of the Spirit and of power: that your faith should not stand in the wisdom of men, but in the power of God. 1 Corinthians 2:1-5

I like this passage; it portrays Paul fixed on Jesus Christ and on the work of the cross. Paul's preaching of the gospel came with a *demonstration of the Spirit and of power*. Not only were souls saved, but people were healed and delivered, and miracles were performed. There was a demonstration of power. Paul downplayed his ability, saying that this demonstration of power was not due to his excellent speaking, but to the work of the Holy Spirit. Why? We see the answer in the last verse—so that man's faith would not stand on the wisdom of men, but in the power of God.

Our faith is so important. Without faith we can do nothing. True faith is not trusting in man, but trusting in the Lord Jesus Christ. What we have today is the slick, fancy, witty and sometimes funny preaching of men enticing the lost into the Kingdom of God. Unfortunately for those hearing the message, they put their faith in the man and not

A Church of Power Is Emerging

the Savior. They see the man more than Jesus. What is the result? A weak conversion, a faith built on man and not on the Rock, a faith that can easily crumble. That's why we have too many Christians today who have backslidden or are still immature, they are looking to man.

For all the preaching, for all the revival meetings, for all the crusades throughout this country of the United States, there is very little lasting fruit; there are very few churches where the lampstand is burning brightly. It has been a long time since we have seen or experienced a great move of God. Why? Because we are missing the Holy Spirit power.

When the preaching comes with a demonstration of power man is more inclined to look to the source of power, Jesus Christ. The outcome can be a life-changing conversion that immediately causes one to be sold out for the Lord. This is the kind of Christian for whom the Lord is looking, one who will remain and bear much fruit.

Let me summarize the point to which we have come in this book. I declared to you as a prophetic word that a Church of power is soon to emerge; that I believe the Church today is lacking the Pentecostal power, the baptism of the Holy Spirit, and anointed preaching followed by healing, signs and wonders.

A Church of Power Is Emerging

We do not often see today a manifestation or demonstration of the Holy Spirit in power. In fact, the Church is denying this supernatural power. We, the Body of Christ, are in error because we do not know the Scriptures nor the power of God. Furthermore, we are in sin because we have missed the mark that the Lord Jesus Christ has set forth for all Christians.

So, how do we get this outpouring of the Holy Spirit that fell on Pentecost? We went to the Word of God to seek God's purpose for this awesome power. We learned that the baptism of the Holy Spirit is to enable us to take action, to specifically preach the gospel, to heal the sick, to cast out demons and to perform miracles, signs and wonders and that without the baptism of the Holy Spirit we are not fully equipped—we lack a supernatural ingredient. These are the actions that a believer should be doing and with the desired result of seeing souls saved. The attitude of our heart, our motive for receiving the Holy Spirit power, should be focused on winning souls into the Kingdom of God. When you have God's purpose in mind, you're on the right track.

2

Who Will Get the Power?

The answer is *disciples*.

Simple enough, isn't it? Those individuals who will experience a mighty outpouring of the Holy Spirit will be disciples of Jesus Christ. The local churches that soon will emerge and be set apart from the others because of the mighty works of God done in their midst will have a people who are *disciples*.

I have another question for you—think of me asking this question of your whole church body at Sunday worship. Do you believe that you are a disciple of Jesus Christ according to the Word of God? Be honest. Don't claim to be something in the sight of God that you are not. You wouldn't want to have to admit, once we begin to study what it means to be a disciple, that in fact you fall short of the Lord's requirement. Please, take some time to think about this.

If you answered yes, you believe that you are a disciple, wait until the end of this chapter to see if you haven't changed your mind. I believe there will be very, very few who will still be able to say yes to this question in the sight of God. Now, if there are a few who can say yes, I am a true disciple of the Lord, I have one more question for you. I direct this question mainly to the pastors and leaders: Why are your people not disciples?

The importance of all this is that Jesus intended that disciples, and disciples alone, be endued with power. Jesus referred to all those who followed Him as His disciples, including the Twelve. Jesus gave power and authority only to His disciples during His earthly ministry. On Pentecost it was His disciples on whom the Holy Spirit fell. Jesus commanded the 11 disciples to go and make disciples of all nations. It would be the disciples who would receive the baptism of the Holy Spirit that would turn the world upside down. It will be churches made up of disciples that will turn the world upside down as we approach the year 2000.

Let us not be too presumptuous as to what a true disciple of the Lord is. As we simply look at the four

The Teachings of Jesus

In the very first Scripture where Jesus was speaking He was but 12 years old. Jesus had gone to Jerusalem with His parents for the Feast of Passover. When the feast was over His parents left, unaware that the boy Jesus had stayed behind in Jerusalem and believing He was with their relatives. Upon finding Him missing, they returned to Jerusalem to find Jesus in the temple courts, sitting among the teachers, listening to them and asking them questions. This is what Jesus said when they found Him: "How is it that ye sought Me? wist ye not that I must be about My Father's business?" (Lk. 2:49) It goes on to say in Luke 2:52, "And Jesus increased in wisdom and stature, and in favor with God and man."

This is an incredible incident, as we consider the age of Jesus. At 12, Jesus was focused on the Father's business and not His own, and He was considered to be increasing in wisdom. My point is that as wise as Jesus was, it would be prudent for us to heed the words of Jesus. If it is pure disciples that we seek to make, let us diligently study the gospels to find out how Jesus turned those who followed Him into disciples who turned the world upside down.

Here is a command of the Lord spoken to the 11 disciples:

> *All power is given unto Me in heaven and in earth. Go ye therefore, and teach all nations, baptizing them in the name of the Father, and of the Son, and of the Holy Ghost: teaching them to observe all things whatsoever I have commanded you: and, lo, I am with you alway, even unto the end of the world.* Matthew 28:18-20
>
> *Therefore go and make disciples of all nations....* Matthew 28:19, NIV
>
> *Going therefore disciple all the nations....* Matthew 28:19, Interlinear Greek-English New Testament[1]

At the same time that Jesus commanded the disciples, "Go ye into all the world, and preach the gospel to every creature" (Mk. 16:15), He also sent them out to teach all nations, to disciple all nations.

The Father's plan was to send His only Son to save the world. But the world was to be saved through Jesus' death and resurrection, not by Jesus Himself going to every lost soul to proclaim the good news. That would be left to His disciples, and this is where you and I become involved. Jesus' task included teaching others to continue in His footsteps. So, for the gospel to be spread throughout the

---

1. George Ricker Berry, *Interlinear Greek-English New Testament* (Nashville: Broadman Press, 1990).

world, it was also necessary for the 11 to properly train others to become disciples. That this might be an effective plan, Jesus said, "...teaching them to observe all things whatsoever I have commanded you...."

Brothers and sisters in Christ, this one Scripture is where the Church has parted company with the teachings of our Lord. Churches today give little thought to the true meaning of *disciple*. Pastors, teachers, evangelists and other leaders often teach whatever they feel led to teach. They teach what they know or what they have been taught at a Bible institute or seminary. But the teachings of men will not do. Jesus said to teach them what "I have commanded you." It is Jesus' teachings, His way of life, His method of making disciples that we should copy.

This chapter is a result of searching and studying the gospels to find out how Jesus made ordinary fishermen into disciples. Believe me when I say this chapter will make a difference in your life. We will learn the *purpose* for being a disciple. We will learn about *attitudes* and the *cost* of being a disciple of the Lord. We will learn what Jesus' *method* of making disciples was. Lastly, we will learn what a real disciple is and whether you pass the discipleship "test."

The Purpose for Being a Disciple

There are many people who have achieved greatness in life, according to man's standards, because of purpose in their life. Dictators have maliciously acquired power and reigned over nations. These dictators had purpose: to become a ruler or a king. Doctors have spent years studying for the purpose of healing mankind. Sports legends have trained for the purpose of being the best at their sport, of going down in the record books. Movie stars and singers have achieved stardom because of purpose in their life. Whether it was fame or fortune or to achieve greatness or otherwise, they had a purpose.

Purpose, as we recall from the previous chapter, is a result which one desires to obtain and which is kept in mind as one performs an action. All these people had a desired result which burned in their mind. Whether one desires to rule, to make the world better, to be the best at what one does or to become famous or rich, it takes a purpose.

Jesus came to earth with a purpose to save the lost from sin, and Jesus trained His disciples so as to give them purpose for becoming one of His disciples.

From that time Jesus began to preach, and to say, Repent: for the kingdom of heaven is at hand. And Jesus, walking by the sea of Galilee, saw two brethren, Simon called Peter, and Andrew his brother, casting a net into the sea: for they were fishers. And He saith unto them, Follow Me, and I will make you fishers of men. Matthew 4:17-19

Who Will Get the Power?

Here is recorded the story in which Jesus invited Peter and his brother Andrew to become His disciples. Jesus said, "Follow Me." The basic definition of a disciple is "one who follows another's teaching." Implicit in Jesus' words *follow Me* was that Peter and Andrew would be taught His doctrines.

At the same time that Peter and Andrew were asked to follow Jesus, they also were told the purpose for becoming His disciples: they were to become fishers of men.

It was not just the Twelve whom Jesus challenged to follow Him.

And He said unto another, Follow Me. But he said, Lord, suffer me first to go and bury my father. Jesus said unto him, Let the dead bury their dead: but go thou and preach the kingdom of God. Luke 9:59-60

Here is another individual whom Jesus challenged to follow Him. Notice that with the words *follow Me* came the purpose: to go and preach the kingdom of God.

Jesus called many others to follow Him. To Philip and Matthew and the rich young ruler He said, "Follow Me." Because we have no Scripture in which He specifically said to these individuals that they would become fishers of men, I believe that Jesus was soon

A Church of Power Is Emerging

to make known to them their purpose for following Him.

The main point of this section is that I believe many Christians today are aimlessly following the Lord with no purpose. They have no understanding that they have been called to follow Jesus Christ in order to be fishers of men. Listen to me, brethren, churches are packed on Sunday with parishioners who are wrapped up in their own problems and thinking about their worldly aspirations, having no knowledge or regard to furthering the Kingdom of God. No one has ever said to them, "Folks, you're here so that we can disciple you for the purpose of going forth and preaching the gospel." That's why churches remain stagnant, many of them gasping for their last breath, because there is no new life. There are no new babes who have come into the Kingdom. These Christians need to know there is a purpose in their life now that they have been saved, and it is not to warm the church pews. It is not to worship on Sunday and go home to watch television. The purpose that Jesus has for all His disciples is to become a fisher of men.

What about our young who go off to Bible college? Do they go to get credentials? Do they go to become a pastor so they can preach from the pulpit? What kind of desire is this? Some seminaries are no better. They teach knowledge, history, traditions, theology and fancy terms. They should be teaching the thirsting Christian how to be a disciple of Jesus Christ. Jesus didn't offer electives for His disciples, He offered a course on discipleship. Jesus didn't offer a degree or credentials to His disciples, He offered them the power of God.

Our colleges and seminaries should be teaching people how to be disciples. They should be driving it into their minds to be fishers of men and teaching them with hands on training how to preach the Kingdom, how to witness, how to win the lost, and how to heal the sick. This should be their focus.

Remember, you are to be a disciple first, before becoming a pastor, teacher, evangelist or any other calling. I am not against Bible colleges and seminaries. I am against teaching inerrant ways that do not line up with the Lord's method of teaching. We need to have the right purpose and a noble desire instilled into the hearts and minds of our young: to go and preach the Kingdom of God.

The Attitude of a Disciple

Those of you who, as I, have taken to following Jesus Christ, whether it has been for a short time or many years, probably will agree that it has been different. Jesus was no ordinary man. His teachings are astonishing, when you think about it, and His methods extraordinary. So to follow Jesus one would expect a whole new way of life. Just how different is your life?

You and I, our fathers, the Israelites, Moses, Abraham and Adam, all were of the dust of the earth, from this world. Our ways, our thinking, our dreams and aspirations all are of this world. Our kingdoms, rules and domains are of this world. Jesus, on the other hand, came from Heaven. He said, "My kingdom is not of this world..." (Jn. 18:36). His ways, His thinking, His teaching and methods all are from Heaven. To follow Jesus is to completely change, to be transformed from earthly to heavenly ways.

One of the first teachings of Jesus was the Sermon on the Mount, recorded in Matthew, chapters 5-7, and in Luke, chapter 6. I personally believe there is significance to the fact Jesus began His teaching of the disciples with this sermon—significance in the sense of where Jesus began His lesson with new disciples. Throughout this sermon there underlies the change a disciple must undergo—a change of attitude, a change from the earthly to the heavenly. What good would it do to train disciples to go out to preach and to heal, to teach and to make other disciples, if their motive was to be rich and famous, if their attitude was to be well fed and clothed, to laugh and have a good time or if they could not forgive and show mercy? They would negate by their actions all that the Word of God had accomplished.

Beloved, Christians need to be challenged from the time they are babes that if they are to follow Jesus Christ, their thinking, attitude and motives must change; their values, focus in life, the rules by which they live and their standard of life all must change.

Consider the beginning of the Sermon on the Mount taken from the Gospel of Luke,

And He lifted up His eyes on His disciples, and said, Blessed be ye poor: for yours is the kingdom of God. Blessed are ye that hunger now: for ye shall be filled. Blessed are ye that weep now: for ye shall laugh. Blessed are ye, when men shall hate you, and when they shall separate you from their company, and shall reproach you, and cast out your name as evil, for the Son of man's sake. Rejoice ye in that day, and leap for joy: for, behold, your reward is great in heaven: for in the like manner did their fathers unto the prophets. But woe unto you that are rich! for ye have received your consolation. Woe unto you that are full! for ye shall hunger. Woe unto you that laugh now! for ye shall mourn and weep. Woe unto you, when all men shall speak well of you! for so did their fathers to the false prophets.
Luke 6:20-26

A Church of Power Is Emerging

First of all, the setting of this passage is on the side of a mountain, from which Jesus addressed a large crowd composed of the 12 apostles, many other disciples and a multitude of others who came to be healed and hear Him teach. Jesus then looked upon His disciples and announced to all those listening that they were blessed. Why were they blessed? Because some had forsaken riches or the pursuit of riches to follow Jesus. They were resolved to living a poor life; there would be no hourly wage, no material compensation, no personal, tangible reward. Their decision was purely a selfless act. Their reward would come at a later time; it would be a heavenly reward.

As a disciple there would be times of hunger and thirsting. Yet better to hunger and thirst for righteousness than for the food of the world. These disciples were blessed because it was far better to go hungry now and be filled in Heaven.

The disciples would weep. Jesus would take them to the poor, the poverty-stricken, to the slums. They would see the helplessness of the people, the cruelty inflicted upon them, the bondage and suffering, the sickness and sorrow. They would see how lost the people were and would weep. But one day, in Heaven, they would laugh.

Lastly, to follow Jesus would cause men to rise up against them. Friends and relatives would turn on them and even hate them and speak evil of them because of the name of Jesus. These disciples had forsaken all their worldly friends to follow Him and proclaim the Kingdom of God. Because of this their reward would be great in the Kingdom of God.

Jesus then turned to the crowd and pronounced woes to those who would choose not to follow Jesus, to those who would seek to gratify themselves with food and drink, riches and laughter. The time would come when they would be judged fairly and receive their just reward; a reward of hungering and thirsting, of mourning and weeping.

As you read this, is Jesus saying to you, "You are blessed," or is Jesus saying, "Woe unto you." Most Christians have never been confronted with the stark contrast between the life they are expected to live as a disciple and the kind of life that the pagans live. Could it be that our leaders live a life that so closely parallels that of the world that it would be impossible for them to preach the way of a disciple's life?

Brothers and sisters in the Lord, I say this for your own good: you must forsake everything and follow Jesus. There are many of you who do not believe that you are rich, but you are. You need to sell your land, you need to sell your extra cars and boats, that the money may be distributed among those in need. Jesus never intended for you to spend your weekends out on the lakes anyway. Some of you have large sums of money in savings accounts and IRAs. Jesus said not to worry about tomorrow. Perhaps this money is put away so that you may retire comfortably. I didn't know Christians were allowed to retire.

How many Christians spend most of their spare time eating, drinking and having fun? How does your table look at dinner? Are there meat and potatoes, vegetables and dessert? Or do you ever go hungry? How often do you go out to eat, while the poor in your church go hungry? How much time do you spend walking through the malls for clothes, for fancy dresses and fine suits, for "cool-looking" jackets and coats? How much time do you spend looking for lost souls? Jesus said, "Take no thought for your life, what ye shall eat, or what ye shall drink; nor yet for your body, what ye shall put on. Is not the life more than meat, and the body than raiment?" (Mt. 6:25).

Then there are those who call themselves Christians who seek after the pleasures of this world, laughter and fun. These are the Christians who at breakfast or luncheon gatherings talk about their jobs, the latest sporting events, their baseball, golf and bowling leagues. They laugh, tell jokes and make sport about women and the things of the world. It is sad; their treasure is of this world because that is where their heart is. Jesus said, "For where your treasure is, there will your heart be also" (Mt. 6:21) and "...out of the abundance of the heart the mouth speaketh" (Mt. 12:34). These men and women speak of worldly things because these things have been abundantly stored up within them, and they flow naturally from their mouths. As for me, I would rather sit alone or surround myself with Christians who want to talk about Jesus, whose deep desire is to go and preach the gospel, to heal the sick and to possess the land.

Throughout Jesus' earthly ministry He continually spoke of heavenly and godly things, of the Kingdom of Heaven, of the Kingdom of God. From the beginning of His ministry Jesus came preaching, "Repent, for the Kingdom of Heaven is near." This was a new concept for those who followed Him. Jesus would often teach and preach on the Kingdom of God. We have in the 13th chapter of Matthew all the beautiful parables of what the Kingdom of Heaven is like. Following are two examples.

> *Again, the kingdom of heaven is like unto treasure hid in a field; the which when a man hath found, he hideth, and for joy thereof goeth and selleth all that he hath, and buyeth that field.*

Again, the kingdom of heaven is like unto a merchant man, seeking goodly pearls: who, when he had found one pearl of great price, went and sold all that he had, and bought it. Matthew 13:44-46

Here the Kingdom of Heaven is likened unto a treasure of great value. Those who understand its value are willing to sell everything to purchase it. This is the attitude of a true disciple—willingness to sell out, to sell everything for the Kingdom of God.

Even after Jesus' death and resurrection He spoke to the disciples of the Kingdom of God. "To whom also He shewed Himself alive after His passion by many infallible proofs, being seen of them forty days, and speaking of the things pertaining to the kingdom of God..." (Acts 1:3). It was natural for Jesus to talk about Heaven; that was His home. We see from this passage that Jesus never ceased speaking of His Father's Kingdom. It was important that Jesus teach His followers all that He could about the things of Heaven, for unless a disciple was willing to leave the things of the world behind, He could never follow the Lord. This attitude must be instilled in the new believer as he steps out to follow Jesus Christ.

As we continue to look upon Jesus and examine His words, the making of a disciple becomes more clear and simple. After Jesus called men to follow

Him, He gave them purpose for their new walk—to become fishers of men. To accomplish this required that the attitude of the individual change. Man's attitude had to completely change from one of looking down to the earth and ground to one of looking up to the sky and Heaven itself. It is with this heavenly attitude, this heavenly way of thinking, that Jesus confronts all who would follow Him.

The Cost of Being a Disciple

In the natural world every goal, every dream, every aspiration, whether it is to exist, to exceed or to excel, has its cost. Every man or woman who has had a goal to excel in sports and play professionally has had to pay the price of hard work, long hours of training, body building and practice. Every farmer with a dream to run his own farm has understood there would be many days of awaking early in the morning and toiling until dusk. Anyone who has started his own business has realized he has to put many more hours of work into his business than he can expect from any employee. The bright young man who goes off to college to become a doctor knows there are years and years of studying before he will earn his degree and be licensed to practice medicine. Likewise the carpenter and mason must go through four to six years of apprenticeship. The mother who stays at home to bring up a family pays a high price to rear her children: washing and sewing and cleaning and cooking for no wages often must make a woman wonder whether it is all worth it. You might want to reflect for a moment about your own life, the cost that you have had to pay for your position at your place of work.

Now, as someone who is saved and has a desire to be a disciple of the Lord, do you believe there is a cost? How costly is it to follow Jesus Christ?

"And He said to them all, If any man will come after Me, let him deny himself, and take up his cross daily, and follow Me" (Lk. 9:23). Notice what is implied here as a precedent to following Jesus. The implication is that one must be willing to deny himself and take up his cross daily if he is to become a disciple. The Church shirks her duty when she doesn't advise all would-be disciples that there is an immediate cost in becoming a disciple.

Too many churches will do anything to build up the size of their following. They never confront the people with words like *repentance* and *cost*. The Church today considers these to be "deadly words" that can cause many people to turn away. Heaven forbid that anyone would walk out of the church! However, it seems to me that I recall many who walked away from the Lord because His teachings were too tough. If the Scripture teaches that we are to deny ourselves, then that is what we need to teach.

Who Will Get the Power?

What exactly does it mean to deny self? To *deny* means to "say no to." As Christians we are both fleshly and spiritual. Our flesh has not disappeared. We still will have countless fleshly desires and thoughts every day. To deny oneself means to make a conscious decision to say *no* to every thought and desire that originates from self.

The complement to denying self is taking up our cross, a life of sacrifice and suffering for the sake of the gospel. We are to do this daily. You cannot say to yourself that you deny yourself for the sake of following Jesus if there is no taking up of the cross. But we will get to that in a moment. The point here is that denying self and taking up the cross daily go together.

Following are some examples of denying self.

You belong to a league that bowls weekly. This event is for leisure and pleasure that is solely for self. Deny it by quitting the league, and don't wait until the end of the season. Consider joining another league whose members go out and preach the gospel.

You work hard all day, come home to rest and then eat dinner. Afterward you head to the livingroom to watch television. Deny yourself, say no and do not turn on the TV. Pick up your Bible, turn to the gospels and find out what Jesus has to say.

A lustful thought and temptation come before you. Say no. Get on your knees, focus your thoughts on Jesus and begin to pray.

In order to deny self, one must constantly examine his own thoughts and actions. Every action involves a decision of which we are in control, because God has given us a free will. We then must make a choice: we either gratify ourselves or we deny ourselves and take up our cross.

The Lord uses some stronger language in the Gospel of John:

And Jesus answered them, saying, The hour is come, that the Son of man should be glorified. Verily, verily, I say unto you, Except a corn of wheat fall into the ground and die, it abideth alone: but if it die, it bringeth forth much fruit. John 12:23-24

Here Jesus gives a parable of hidden truth regarding His life—that for His ministry and teaching to bear much fruit, first He must die and then be resurrected. In order for Jesus to be glorified, first must come death and then the resurrection. The same is true for every man or woman who would take up his or her cross and follow Jesus. First, we must die, and we must be buried.

The Christian who would follow the Lord must not only deny himself, but die to self—to self-will, self-pride, self-centeredness, self-gratification. Every deed, activity and thought of pleasure and lust, every bad habit that is connected with self must die.

We die to self by surrendering ourselves completely to God, confessing our sins, repenting of them and trusting in Christ's death as the atonement for our sins. Once we have died, we can then begin to bear fruit by allowing the resurrection power of the Holy Spirit to transform us into the image of Christ.

We learned that our purpose as a disciple is to fish for men, to proclaim the gospel. The above Scripture passage implies that there is force in our proclamation, that there is strength in our testimony, when we have died, that in fact there is no strength or force to our testimony of Jesus Christ when self still lives.

How many Christians occasionally witness with seemingly no effect? How many pastors preach and teach with no effect, with no force or strength, with no anointing? Why is this? Because they have not died to self. Brothers and sisters, again I say to you that only disciples of Jesus Christ will be anointed with power. Jesus said, "Go, and make disciples." A disciple is one whom the Lord expects to deny self and to die to self. Only then can you ever expect to be endued with power.

Suffering is not a very nice word, is it? Who likes to suffer? The expression *take up your cross* was synonymous with a life of suffering. These are the words that our Lord spoke about the apostle Paul:

Go thy way: for he is a chosen vessel unto Me, to bear My name before the Gentiles, and kings, and the children of Israel: For I will shew him how great things he must suffer for My name's sake. Acts 9:15-16

Paul would suffer for the name of Jesus. In Second Corinthians 11:23-27, we have an account of all that Paul went through:

Are they ministers of Christ? (I speak as a fool) I am more; in labours more abundant, in stripes above measure, in prisons more frequent, in deaths oft. Of the Jews five times received I forty stripes save one. Thrice was I beaten with rods, once was I stoned, thrice I suffered shipwreck, a night and a day I have been in the deep; in journeyings often, in perils of waters, in perils of robbers, in perils by mine own countrymen, in perils by the heathen, in perils in the city, in perils in the wilderness, in perils in the sea, in perils among false brethren; in weariness and painfulness, in watchings often, in hunger and thirst, in fastings often, in cold and nakedness

We are not in a contest, as a disciple, to see who can suffer the most. What is important is to know that, yes, a disciple is expected to go through times of suffering. "For unto you it is given in the behalf of Christ, not only to believe on Him, but also to suffer for His sake..." (Phil. 1:29). Christianity does not end with believing in Jesus Christ. Christianity goes on to a life of suffering.

One of the many perils the apostle Paul faced was the peril in the city. Throughout the world, in many of our cities perils lurk on every street corner. Drugs, alcohol, prostitution, street gangs, robbery and murder abound in the heart of the city. Who dares to go with the gospel into these black holes where not even a glimmer of the light of Christ shines? This is where the poor live. This is where sin abounds and the lost are gathered. Christians back away in fear and intimidation. Oh! Where is there a Christian who would suffer for Jesus' name sake? Where is there a Christian who would enter the lions' den to proclaim the gospel?

If you truly desire to be a disciple, take this chapter to heart. Denying self, dying to self and suffering for His name are not electives in our walk with the Lord. They are requirements.

Jesus' Method of Making Disciples

We began this chapter with the statement that it would be disciples who would receive the power, who would be anointed with the Holy Spirit. Truly, our desire should be to see a demonstration of the Holy spirit and power in our life, but more so to live in obedience to the Lord. Our desire should be to

A Church of Power Is Emerging

become a real disciple of Jesus Christ according to the Word of God. Our desire as leaders in the local churches also should be to make real disciples of all who profess the name of Christ.

Just how do you make a disciple? The truest and most perfect way would be to look at the life of Christ and learn how He discipled those who followed Him. There is no doubt that these men turned the world upside down. This is proof that Jesus' method of making disciples worked.

Where did Jesus begin? He began with two simple words, "Follow Me." The word *disciple* may be defined as "one who follows another's teaching." But here we get caught up with the word *teaching*, which in our present-day society and social church system indicates classroom training. Jesus did not say to Peter, Andrew, Matthew, Philip and other disciples to "come and be a disciple of Me." No, He said, "Follow Me." Literally to follow someone is to walk behind or near to and observe and learn all that the teacher says and does. This was Jesus' method of teaching—on-the-job training. It was on the dirt roads, on the hillsides and along the shores that those who followed Jesus would soon learn what the life of a disciple was like.

There are many tasks in life that are best taught by example, by doing them in front of those whom we are teaching. Sewing, cooking, ironing, hammering a nail, sawing wood and chopping down a tree with an ax all are best taught to others as they watch. The delicate and intricate work of surgery can best be learned by observing another surgeon and practicing and trying to duplicate his work. How much more delicate is the soul than the body! We should not take the souls of the lost lightly. The soul is eternal. Should we then not use the method of Jesus, a perfect method, and teach others by letting them follow us?

Now let us look at some foundation blocks in Jesus' method of teaching. To follow the Master would be to adopt the same purpose for which Jesus traveled about. "For the Son of man is come to seek and to save that which was lost" (Lk. 19:10). If nothing else, the disciples would learn the love and compassion that Jesus had for the lost, the tremendous desire to see them saved. Notice that Jesus had to seek them out; He went out to preach the good news.

I don't understand the belief in our churches today that somehow these lost souls are going to come wandering into our sanctuaries, the belief that as we stay within the confines of our church buildings the lost will get saved. This doesn't seem to be *seeking the lost*. But going into the inner city, to neighborhoods where the people congregate on the

A Church of Power Is Emerging

streets and in parks, to the market places and house to house would seem to be seeking out the lost. Where is our love for the lost souls?

To follow Jesus would be to learn the message of salvation. At first the disciples would hear Jesus proclaim, "Repent, for the Kingdom of Heaven is near." Repentance was a key. In Mark 6:12, we see that the disciples went out and preached similarly. "And they [the disciples] went out, and preached that men should repent." Later, after His death and resurrection, again Jesus explained "that repentance and remission of sins should be preached in His name..." (Lk. 24:47) and said to the disciples, "...and ye shall be witnesses unto Me..." (Acts 1:8). Remission of sins could now be preached because of the work of the cross. Also they were to be witnesses to Jesus' being alive, to His resurrection from the grave, which proved that He was who He claimed to be, the Son of God. This was the basic message of salvation which the disciples were taught and commanded to preach.

To follow Jesus would be to learn not only what the message was, but how to proclaim this message. The disciples watched Jesus as He ministered to the paralytic, to the rich young ruler, to Zacchaeus, to Nicodemus, to the Samaritan woman at the well, to the blind man, to the lepers and to the woman caught in adultery. To the paralytic Jesus proclaimed forgiveness of sins; to the rich young ruler, how to get eternal life; to Zacchaeus, repentance; to Nicodemus, "you must be born again;" to the blind man, believe in the Son of man; to the Samaritan woman, living water; and to the woman caught in adultery, leave your life of sin.

Jesus ministered differently to each of those with whom He would come into contact, but one thing was clear from listening to Him: the heart of His message was salvation. There was much that the disciples would learn as Jesus fed the multitudes, ate with the tax collectors and sinners, raised Lazarus from the dead and from the many other examples not recorded in the Bible.

It was from a comfortable place in Heaven that Jesus was sent to the earth, a world where satan was roaming about seeking to devour, kill and maim. From a spiritual standpoint the world was not the safest and best place to be. But it would be in the world that Jesus would train His disciples and later send them out to preach the gospel. It is in the world that real discipleship takes place.

More than ever before, the gospel needs to be taken to the streets. We don't need any more leaders who teach from the pulpit and from the front of classrooms; rather we need leaders who can disciple others in proclaiming the gospel in the highways and byways. This is where disciples are made.

A Church of Power Is Emerging

Not long ago I was walking with my good brother in the Lord, Patrick, along the shore of the lake not too far from where I live. This we often would do as we spoke of the teachings of Jesus. This particular day as we walked from the pier, I looked up to see we were in the midst of a carnival. There before us was a stand where you had to throw a basketball into the hoop to win a prize. We stood there for a while and watched young and old try to throw the ball through the net. No one succeeded.

Then the attendant of the booth came forward to show everyone how it was done. In three short tries the ball went up, bounced lightly around and fell through the hoop. I noticed the difference between his method of throwing the ball and that of those who had failed. The attendant had thrown the ball in an underhand fashion so that the ball would gently reach the basket and then bounce around and finally fall in. Everyone else had thrown the ball overhanded, thus it would reach the basket rather speedily and bounce right off with no chance of going in.

"Aha!" I said, after watching the attendant, "this is the correct way to make the basket." Now you would think that someone would follow this man who obviously was quite experienced, if they wanted to win the prize. Wrong! I watched in amazement as all those who had watched this man make the basket continued to throw in their same way. They wasted all their money never to walk home with a prize. What a lesson for me as I watched. This, I thought, was a perfect example of the Body of Christ. Following the Master through the Word, we have the perfect way to win the prize, to go out and win souls and to heal the sick. Yet, we are so stubborn as to think that our ways are better, that today's method of making disciples works better than the Lord's. So on we go in our old ways.

To follow Jesus would be to exercise one's faith. The gospels are filled with examples of Jesus coming face to face with the diseased, the sick, the lame, the blind and the demon possessed. Either Jesus was the Son of God with the power to heal the sick and bring deliverance, or He was just another man. But Jesus exercised the authority and power given to Him and healed all those who were brought to Him. Yes, He was the Son of God.

The disciples, after watching Jesus over and over again as He healed the sick, then were given power and authority and ordered to go out and do likewise. They were to exercise their faith. Beloved, the Scripture says, "For we walk by faith, not by sight..." (2 Cor. 5:7). A Christian is one whose daily life is an exercise in faith. It is following the life of Christ, not the life of our leaders. It is in walking, not sitting in church pews, that we exercise our faith. It is in laying our hands on the sick that we exercise our faith, not in wondering to which doctor we need to take someone. It is in casting out demons in the name of Jesus that we exercise our faith. Yes, faith is a gift, and it comes by grace. But we need to nurture every ounce of faith that the Lord has given us.

Recall the story about the barren fig tree

Now in the morning as He returned into the city, He hungered. And when He saw a fig tree in the way, He came to it, and found nothing thereon, but leaves only, and said unto it, Let no fruit grow on thee henceforward for ever. And presently the fig tree withered away. And when the disciples saw it, they marvelled, saying, How soon is the fig tree withered away! Jesus answered and said unto them, Verily I say unto you, If ye have faith, and doubt not, ye shall not only do this which is done to the fig tree, but also if ye shall say unto this mountain, Be thou removed, and be thou cast into the sea; it shall be done. And all things, whatsoever ye shall ask in prayer, believing, ye shall receive. Matthew 21:18-22

The Christian today is knowledgeable about the fact that with God all things are possible and that we can say to the mountain, "Be thou removed," and it will be removed. But how many Christians have actually said to a mountain, "Be thou removed," and experienced the removal of the mountain? Have you?

Jesus meant for every disciple to exercise his faith. We walk by faith. Faith without deeds is dead. It is exercising our faith that pleases God. The disciples watched in amazement as Jesus calmed the waters, as He cast out demons and raised the dead. With all the books on faith, with all the seminars and teachings on faith, we still have a body of Christians who lack faith. Why? Because there is no one to say to new Christians, "Come and follow me, I will teach you the ways of Jesus Christ and exhort you to exercise your faith."

A Real Disciple

I had always been of the belief that when you were born again you became a disciple of Jesus Christ. Maybe you believe this too. When we go to the Word of God, we should have a teachable spirit that searches for the truth. Many times the truth has hurt me; it has hurt my feelings, my pride, my ego, and it has demolished doctrines that have been ingrained within me. But Jesus said, "And ye shall know the truth, and the truth shall make you free" (Jn. 8:32). It is time for many Christians to come to know the truth and to be set free.

Following are the words of Jesus in John 8:31:

Then Jesus said to those Jews which believed on Him, If ye continue in My word, then are ye My disciples indeed.... KJV

If you hold to My teaching, you are really My disciples. NIV

If you obey My teaching you are really My disciples.... TEV

If ye abide in My word, truly My disciples ye are. Greek Interlinear New Testament

The Christian walk begins with believing in Jesus Christ. Discipleship begins with the words *"Come, follow Me"* and doing so. A real disciple, however, is a Christian who not only begins to follow the teachings of Jesus, but continues in His Word, holds to His teaching; obeys His teaching and abides in His Word.

Discipleship is a continual process. It never ends. A real disciple doesn't give up on Jesus. Yes, there will be times of doubt and lack of faith, of fear and solitude. Amidst all the troubled times our response will be like Peter's, "Lord, to whom shall we go? Thou hast the words of eternal life. And we believe and are sure that Thou art that Christ, the Son of the living God" (Jn. 6:68-69).

Discipleship holds to the teaching of Jesus. Again, it is the teaching of Jesus and, most specifically, the words recorded in the gospels that pertain to the making of a disciple and more so to Jesus' method of making disciples, which turns a Christian into a praying, devil-stomping, soul-winning disciple.

Listen carefully, brothers and sisters, most of you, I repeat, most of you are following the teachings of your pastor and your pastor's method of making disciples, which do not line up with the teachings of Jesus. The main reason for this is a lack of the fivefold ministry in the Body of Christ. (We will discuss this in the following chapters.) The result is a congregation of believers who never mature into disciples. Friends, Jesus wants you to be a disciple.

A real disciple obeys the teaching of Jesus. At the end of the Gospel of Matthew Jesus told the apostles to go and make disciples and teach them to observe (obey) the commands of Jesus. Obedience is a key word throughout the Scriptures, from beginning to end, from the command to Adam not to eat from the tree of the knowledge of good and evil to the command to the apostles to preach the gospel to the ends of the earth. Jesus taught much on obedience. The first and lengthiest teaching of Jesus is the Sermon on the Mount, recorded in Matthew 5-7. Jesus ended the sermon with a teaching on obedience:

Therefore whosoever heareth these sayings of Mine, and doeth them, I will liken him unto a wise man, which built his house upon a rock: and the rain descended, and the floods came, and the winds blew, and beat upon that house; and it fell not: for it was founded upon a rock. And every one that heareth these sayings of Mine, and doeth them not, shall be likened unto a foolish man, which built his house upon the sand: and the rain descended, and the floods came, and the winds blew, and beat upon that house; and it fell: and great was the fall of it. Matthew 7:24-27

It is foolishness, utter folly, to read the gospels and teachings of Jesus and not do them. All the words spoken by our Lord in these three chapters of Matthew need to be taken to heart, meditated upon and then acted out. The same applies to the rest of the teachings of Jesus.

Following is an example of the foolishness of many of our church leaders. Jesus spoke in response to all the wickedness He saw being carried on in His Father's house, "It is written, *My house shall be called the house of prayer*; but ye have made it a den of thieves" (Mt. 21:13 emphasis added). Many pastors and church leaders to whom I have spoken have been convicted by this passage and have preached over and over on this Scripture, yet they have failed to obey and do what the Word says! The house in which their people gather still remains prayerless. How sad.

Who Will Get the Power?

Many churches invite traveling evangelists to come and speak. The evangelist chastises them for their lack of soul winning and then exhorts them to go forth and preach the gospel. In response, Christians come to the altar and cry out to God, yet little fruit ever comes forth from the Word. The church remains stagnant with no evangelistic thrust. Our cities still are lost and in the grip of satan. It is obedience that the Lord requires. Be a wise disciple and do what the Lord says.

This next passage should be a warning to all who profess to be disciples.

While He yet talked to the people, behold, His mother and His brethren stood without, desiring to speak with Him. Then one said unto Him, Behold, Thy mother and Thy brethren stand without, desiring to speak with Thee. But He answered and said unto him that told Him, Who is My mother? and who are My brethren? And He stretched forth His hand toward His disciples, and said, Beyond My mother and My brethren! For whosoever shall do the will of My Father which is in heaven, the same is My brother, and sister, and mother. Matthew 12:46-50

How sad this scripture is! Here Mary, the mother of Jesus, whom the Bible tells us was blessed, was excluded from among those who were close to

Him. Be warned, there are many men in high church positions who presume that because of their position they are in a close relationship with the Lord and are doing His will. One day the Lord again will stretch forth His hand and point out His true disciples.

Let us more clearly state what the Lord meant by being His disciple. What is a real disciple? A real disciple is a born-again Christian who has taken to following Jesus Christ. He or she knows that their main purpose while on this earth is to witness, to preach the gospel and to seek and to save the lost. Their attitude has changed from one of being focused on the world to one of forsaking the world's pleasures and riches for the ways of Jesus. A real disciple is focused on heavenly ways—involving hungering, weeping, persecution and humility.

A real disciple has counted the cost of following Jesus and has made a decision to go all the way, to deny everything that gratifies self, to take up his cross daily and to count it a blessing to suffer for the name of Jesus. A real disciple has been discipled according to Jesus' method of hands-on experience in preaching the gospel, healing the sick and casting out demons. No classroom experience will suffice, only real-life experiences to the point where you are capable to go forth two by two. A real disciple continues in the teaching of Jesus, diligently studying the Scriptures, obeying all the commands of Jesus and putting into practice what he or she has learned. This is what a real disciple is like.

Discipleship Test

We began this chapter by asking the question, "Do you believe that you are a disciple of Jesus Christ according to the Word of God?" This may not be as simple to answer as it was before you started to read through this chapter. I would hope that this chapter has given you a new perspective on the meaning of discipleship. The intention was not to lower the esteem of any Christian nor to demean any teachings in the Church today, but to bring us Christians into maturity. The time is soon coming for a great work of the Lord. It is important that each of us be ready.

The teaching in this chapter may have seemed hard to you, but the teachings of Jesus were hard to many who followed Him. Here is an example from the Gospel of John:

> *Then Jesus said unto them, Verily, verily I say unto you, Except ye eat the flesh of the Son of man, and drink His blood, ye have no life in you.... Many therefore of His disciples, when they had heard this, said, This is an hard saying; who can hear it?...From that time many of His disciples went back, and walked no more with Him.*
> John 6:53,60,66

If we were to read on we would find only the Twelve remained to follow Jesus. Take a moment and reflect on this. Imagine that you are the pastor of a large congregation. You are convicted to preach a very hard sermon on Sunday, which leaves your followers having to make a decision to be sold out for Jesus Christ and totally deny themselves and their life style. You then tell them everyone will be going out into the streets to proclaim the gospel starting next Sunday. When the next Sunday comes, 15 minutes after the service begins you look out over your congregation and count 12 persons, one of whom is your wife and three of whom are your children. You might say to yourself, "What have I done?"

Pastor, how often have you struggled with this problem? Maybe you have pressure from the other leaders, board members, or those with money who are out to build the biggest congregation in town. You may use the latest marketing techniques to advertise your church and attract new members. Maybe you have similar hopes and similar thinking yourself. So you water down the Word of God; you compromise the Word of God, even believing in a new gospel for today and a new 20th-century discipleship program. Pastor, no doubt you are under tremendous pressure from the established church system, but remember, one day you will stand before God.

Who Will Get the Power?

One day all of us will stand before God and give an account. I want the Lord to point to me and say, "Behold, my good and faithful servant. He was a true disciple." Will the Lord speak this way of you? Only you can answer the question as to whether you are a disciple of the Lord indeed. To help you scripturally judge for yourself as to how far you have come with the Lord, I would like to share the following passage with you.

And it came to pass, that, as they went in the way, a certain man said unto Him, Lord, I will follow Thee withersoever Thou goest. And Jesus said unto him, Foxes have holes, and birds of the air have nests; but the Son of man hath not where to lay His head. And He said unto another, Follow Me. but he said, Lord, suffer me first to go and bury my father. Jesus said unto him, Let the dead bury their dead: but go thou and preach the kingdom of God. And another also said, Lord, I will follow Thee; but let me first go bid them farewell, which are at home at my house. And Jesus said unto him, No man, having put his hand to the plough, and looking back, is fit for the kingdom of God. After these things the Lord appointed other seventy also, and sent them two and two before His face into every city and place, whither He Himself would come. Therefore said He unto them, The harvest truly is great, but the labourers are few: pray ye therefore the Lord of the harvest, that He would send forth labourers into His harvest. Luke 9:57-10:2

I believe that there were many, maybe hundreds of people, who followed the Lord, listened to His words and were amazed with His deeds. Yet, when it came time to pass the discipleship test, the Lord appointed only 70 other than the Twelve to go and proclaim the Kingdom of God. Only a few who chose to follow Jesus matured to the point where they were fit for service in the Kingdom of God and committed enough to leave everything behind to go and preach the Kingdom of God. Many who sought to follow Jesus found they had an excuse not to totally commit themselves. They had other commitments, other works that were more important. Some who followed Jesus probably were willing to do most anything that the Lord would ask, except preach the gospel. The fact is, as Jesus Himself stated, the laborers are few. It is amazing that 2,000 years later, with millions purporting to be Christians, we still have few laborers to go out into the harvest field.

Where do you stand? Are you one of the few laborers who are out preaching and witnessing to the good news or are you one of the many who stand by and watch? Since our main purpose as a disciple is to fish for men, how can any Christian claim to be a real disciple who has never gone out preaching? This is a true test for any Christian as to whether he or she has matured into a disciple.

Some of you reading through this book may be asking yourself the question, "How do I become a real disciple? Who is there to equip me, to give me hands-on training, so that I can develop into a disciple?" We will shortly come to that. However, you must make an honest appraisal of your life before God and answer the question whether you are a true disciple of Jesus Christ. This is important because I believe there will soon be a great outpouring of the Holy Spirit that will endue disciples with power to go and preach the gospel, to heal the sick and to cast out demons. We Christians need to be prepared for the work of the Lord.

3

The Foundation of the Church

Where Have We Gone Astray?

Christians today are searching for a Church of power. Christians who have been touched for eternity by the Holy Spirit are hungering and thirsting to be a part of a congregation that's on fire for the Lord and where the power of God is being manifested with signs and wonders. So these believers go from church to church hoping to find such a place, only to have their hopes and dreams smashed. Where is this Church of prayer? Where is this Church that seeks God, that preaches repentance, that is looking for a great harvest of souls? Where is this Church of holiness that fears God and keeps His commands? Where is this Church that manifests the power of God?

The prophet Jeremiah received this word:

Then the word of the Lord came unto me, saying, Before I formed thee in the belly I knew thee; and before thou camest forth out of the womb I sanctified thee, and I ordained thee a prophet unto the nations. Then said I, Ah, Lord God! behold, I cannot speak: for I am a child. But the Lord said unto me, Say not, I am a child: for thou shalt go to all that I shall send thee, and whatsoever I command thee thou shalt speak. Be not afraid of their faces: for I am with thee to deliver thee, saith the Lord. Then the Lord put forth His hand, and touched my mouth. And the Lord said unto me, Behold, I have put My words in thy mouth. See, I have this day set thee over the nations and over the kingdoms, to root out, and to pull down, and to destroy, and to throw down, to build, and to plant. Jeremiah 1:4-10

Jeremiah was appointed by God to uproot and pull down, to destroy and to throw down nations and kingdoms. God needs Jeremiahs today who will root out, pull down, destroy and overthrow every stronghold the enemy has set up in Christ's Body,

The Foundation of the Church

everything that exalts itself over the Lord Jesus Christ, who then will build and plant a foundation on Jesus Christ in accordance with and in obedience to His Word, who will build and plant a Church for which Christ Himself is coming back, a Church of power.

Our Father in Heaven is a God of love and mercy. Yet, when it comes to sin, God must expose the sin in His people. Just open some of the prophetic books in the Bible to see how sharply and accurately the Lord's prophets spoke against sin. The Lord's motive for exposing sin is that His children whom He loves would not have to experience His anger and wrath and judgment. We are living in a day when God is speaking through His prophets, warning His people that if this nation does not turn from its wicked ways there will be a swift and furious judgment upon this land. Brothers and sisters in the Lord, the way to prevent judgment upon this nation will only come through the Church, the Bride of Christ. I invite you to open your heart and let God's Word come in.

Jeremiah was referred to as the "weeping prophet." Jeremiah was committed to holiness. He preached repentance unto the people lest their holy city of Jerusalem be destroyed. Because of his doom and gloom preaching and bold proclamation of the unwelcomed truth of impending captivity, he was persecuted by his own people. Today we have a few of those doom and gloom prophets, and no one is listening to them either.

Let's read Jeremiah 8:4-12 (NIV):

Say to them, "This is what the Lord says: 'When men fall down, do they not get up? When a man turns away, does he not return? Why then have these people turned away? Why does Jerusalem always turn away? They cling to deceit; they refuse to return. I have listened attentively, but they do not say what is right. No one repents of his wickedness, saying,"What have I done?" Each pursues his own course like a horse charging into battle. Even the stork in the sky knows her appointed seasons, and the dove, the swift and the thrush observe the time of their migration. But My people do not know the requirements of the Lord. 'How can you say, "We are wise, for we have the law of the Lord," when actually the lying pen of the scribes has handled it falsely? The wise will be put to shame; they will be dismayed and trapped. Since they have rejected the word of the Lord, what kind of wisdom do they have? Therefore I will give their wives to other men and their fields to new owners. From the least to the greatest, all are greedy for gain; prophets and priests alike, all practice deceit. They dress the wound of My people as though it were not serious. "Peace, peace," they say, when there is no peace. Are they ashamed of their loathsome conduct? No, they have no shame at all; they do not even know how to blush. So they fall among the fallen; they will be brought down when they are punished, says the Lord."'

From this passage, we see a people who have turned away from God and refuse to repent. Instead of knowing the requirements of the Lord, each pursues his own course. The prophets speak, yet the people reject the Word of the Lord. Even the greatest, the prophets and priests, led the way in deceitfulness, all greedy for gain.

Ask yourself, "Does this seem like a reflection of the Church today?"

We should also ask ourselves, "Have we, the Body of Christ, turned away from God? Have we the people of the United States turned away from God?"

Consider that prayer has been taken out of our schools; orators are ashamed to use the Word of God in their speeches and compromise the Word of God for the sake of being elected and furthering their political aspirations. Consider the passiveness toward sin that exists, the nudity and profane language on television for all our children to hear, the acceptance of divorce and adultery and the crude killing of unborn babies for the sake of pleasure and convenience. Yes, I believe this country has abruptly turned its back on the Lord.

Does anyone dare question himself and say, "What have I done?" Does any church dare ask itself, "Where have we gone astray?" Does anyone repent? Do we just continue to pursue our own way on a course of destruction?

A System of Error

Sin has become even more deeply rooted in the Body of Christ than one would think. Satan believes that if he can attack the very foundation on which Christianity stands, he might one day topple the Church. The following Scripture lately has been looked at intently by many Christians. We will soon look at this passage, Ephesians 4:10-16, very closely in the King James Version, but right now let us read the Interlinear Greek-English Version.

He that descended is the same also who ascended above all the heavens, that He might fill all things; and He gave some apostles, and some prophets, and some evangelists, and some shepherds and teachers, with a view to the perfecting of the saints; for work of the service, for building up of the body of the Christ; until we all may arrive at the unity of the faith and of the knowledge of the Son of God, at a full-grown man, at the measure of the stature of the fulness of the Christ; that no longer we may be infants, being tossed and carried about by every wind of the teaching in the sleight of men, in craftiness with a view to the systematizing of error; but holding the truth in love we may grow up into Him in all things, who is the head, the Christ: from whom all the body, fitted together and compacted by every joint of supply according to the working in its measure of each one part, the increase of the body makes for itself to the building up of itself in love.

Consider the words *with a view to the perfecting of the saints* and *with a view to the systematizing of error*. This passage depicts the Lord giving apostles, prophets, evangelists, shepherds and teachers as gifts to the Body of Christ when He ascended to Heaven. These gifted people had a view to the perfecting of the saints. Yet, there were other men who came with a view to the setting up of a system of error.

Beloved, you may not believe me, but many of today's denominational and nondenominational churches have established a system of error within them. (We will be more specific later in this book.) This system has become deeply rooted and hinders the working of the Holy Spirit within our local bodies.

Note the constant conflict between Jesus and the Jewish leaders in the gospels.

Then the Pharisees and scribes asked Him, Why walk not Thy disciples according to the tradition of the elders, but eat bread with unwashen hands? He answered and said unto them, Well hath Esaias prophesied of you hypocrites, as it is written, This people honoureth Me with their lips, but their heart is far from Me. Howbeit in vain do they worship Me, teaching for doctrines the commandments of men. For laying aside the commandment of God, ye hold the tradition of men, as the washing of pots and cups: and many other such like things ye do. And He said unto them, Full well ye reject the commandment of God, that ye may keep your own tradition. Mark 7:5-9

The Jews had grown farther and farther away from their God, as evidenced by their setting up their own rules and regulations. The Jews established their own traditions. When Jesus came, He spoke ill of their traditions, seeking to crush them. He began a new work founded upon a "rock."

Without revival man reverts to the old nature. A system of error easily is established when man-made rules and regulations become more important than Christ's rules and the Word of God. Works and man's efforts replace faith in God. But great moves of God have been marked by men confronting the existing church doctrines, as was the case with the Reformation. Likewise, today's church system will be challenged with a new work led by apostles and prophets with a view to the perfecting of the saints for the work of the ministry.

A Pattern for the Church

Our Father in Heaven is not someone who casually and carelessly builds His Church.

Consider Noah's ark. These are the words that God spoke to Noah:

Make thee an ark of gopher wood; rooms shalt thou make in the ark, and shalt pitch it within and without with pitch. And this is the fashion which thou shalt make it of: The length of the ark shall be three hundred cubits, the breadth of it fifty cubits, and the height of it thirty cubits. A window shalt thou make to the ark, and in a cubit shalt thou finish it above; and the door of the ark shalt thou set in the side thereof; with lower, second, and third stories shalt thou make it.
Genesis 6:14-16

God was about to rid the earth of all mankind except for a handful of people whom He chose to save. For God's plan to work, Noah had to build an ark according to the pattern set before him. Now, you might want to ask yourself, "What if Noah had decided to make a few changes to the ark on his own? What if he had decided to change the length and width? Would there have been any change in the outcome to this story as recorded in the Scriptures?" This is a good question worth thinking about. We see that Noah built the ark exactly as he had been commanded, "Thus did Noah; according to all that God commanded him, so did he" (Gen. 6:22).

Remember too the tabernacle. The Lord spoke to Moses, "And let them make Me a sanctuary; that I may dwell among them. According to all that I shew thee, after the pattern of the tabernacle, and the pattern of all the instruments thereof, even so shall ye make it" (Ex. 25:8-9). What an exciting time for Moses and the Israelites. God would actually come down and live among them. Yet, our Lord was very particular about His dwelling place, giving to Moses a specific pattern by which to fashion the tabernacle. We see the meticulous instructions that Moses received when we read on in the Book of Exodus. We may never fully understand the Lord's ways and the importance of building the tabernacle exactly according to the pattern, but I am sure the Lord had a good reason.

The Body of Christ is the Lord's tabernacle on earth today. "...for ye are the temple of the living God..." (2 Cor. 6:16). I believe our Lord, who gave specific instructions in the building of the ark and

The Foundation of the Church

the tabernacle, is just as meticulous and concerned with the building of His Church. For every local church God has a plan that has been laid out in Heaven, and it is of extreme importance that it be copied exactly. Part of the building plan was for the foundation of the church, upon which everything else stands. We should not take lightly the laying of that foundation. Please, have an open mind and heart as we continue our study.

A Look at the Foundation of the Church

Let us imagine going for a drive to look at some of our local churches. We begin our trip by driving through the countryside. As we enter a small village, there by the roadside sits a picture-perfect, postcard-like church. It's a quaint little white church with a steeple on top. We see many similar churches in the country, and we think of a people who gather on Sunday where everyone knows one another and a new visitor would readily be spotted.

Traveling now toward the city we pass through a suburb and notice a huge, modern-looking building with paneled glass around much of the church and a large cross rising up in front. Added buildings linked to the main sanctuary would indicate this church runs a school, possibly from kindergarten through 12th grade.

A Church of Power Is Emerging

As we continue our drive into the heart of the city, we find an altogether different style church. We see an old cathedral with stone walls and fancy stained-glass windows. Inside are the old wooden pews and a monstrous pipe organ that when played shakes the adjacent buildings.

What type of church did you get married in? Was it one similar to any of these? You may be partial to the church you attend for sentimental reasons or because of its looks. You may attend a church because of its school or its children's or youth program.

All of these churches that we just mentioned can be attractive and appealing to us for one reason or another. But as we look at the exterior of the building we can easily be misled concerning the actual construction and condition of the church. Do these churches have a foundation? If they do, what kind of foundation lies under the exterior portion of the churches we looked at? Will these churches stand when the winds and storms come?

Many churches are in such terrible spiritual shape they are ready to collapse. Why are many churches in the condition they are today? Why is there no power in the Church? The answer, I believe, for the most part lies in the foundation. This Scripture from the Gospel of Luke will give us some insight:

The Foundation of the Church

And why call ye Me, Lord, Lord, and do not the things which I say? Whosoever cometh to Me, and heareth My sayings, and doeth them, I will shew you to whom he is like: he is like a man which built an house, and digged deep, and laid the foundation on a rock: and when the flood arose, the stream beat vehemently upon that house, and could not shake it: for it was founded upon a rock. But he that heareth, and doeth not, is like a man that without a foundation built an house upon the earth; against which the stream did beat vehemently, and immediately it fell; and the ruin of that house was great. Luke 6:46-49

The house that withstood the flood was the one built on a solid foundation. The churches that will be able to stand against winds and storms and floods will be the churches built on a solid foundation.

The house that was built upon earth with no foundation collapsed and was destroyed when the flood came. Listen carefully and do not be deceived, brethren. The floods and winds and storms have already come upon the Body of Christ, to local churches, so strongly that some have buckled under the weight of the water and collapsed. I'm talking about the heart of the Church; I'm talking about Jesus Christ and the work of the cross, of the resurrection and of the preaching of the gospel. I'm not talking about the exterior structure or looks or fixtures.

A Church of Power Is Emerging

All of the churches we visited on our little drive had foundations which were well concealed. You could not tell by driving past them whether they had a foundation at all. You could even stop and attend the Sunday service, look around at the four church walls and all the fixtures within, listen to the homily by the well-groomed pastor who preached in his loving and eloquent style, and just marvel at what a great place you are in. You may easily be deceived for you don't even know whether there is a foundation to this local church.

In building, everything depends on a solid foundation. This is especially true with our modern highrise buildings. It is most important that architects calculate accurately the total weight of the building, plus the stress and strain that can come from violent winds, earthquakes and the like. The foundation must be laid accordingly, so that the building will stand under all circumstances.

Similarly, it is extremely necessary that gifted men lay a strong foundation for the local church, for surely the devil will cause stress and strain to fall upon every local church to render it powerless. Does your local church have a foundation? Did the founders dig down deep to lay the foundation upon solid rock? Or is your church set upon the ground?

Has the Foundation of the Church Already Been Laid?

Before continuing our study on the foundation of the Church, we must answer the question: "Has the foundation of the Church already been laid?"

This, beloved, is a crucial point for the Church to consider. For if the foundation of the Church must be laid at the founding of every new local church, then we must ask ourselves, "How is the foundation to be laid?" Furthermore, if we have allowed the careless establishing of new churches for hundreds of years, then in what condition is the Church today?

Many Christians have been taught or are of the opinion that the foundation of the church was properly laid by Jesus Christ and the apostles we read about in the Scriptures. First Corinthians 3:11 is often cited, "For other foundation can no man lay than that is laid, which is Jesus Christ."

Let's look at this passage.

For we are labourers together with God: ye are God's husbandry, ye are God's building. According to the grace of God which is given unto me, as a wise masterbuilder, I have laid the foundation, and another buildeth thereon. But let every man take heed how he buildeth thereupon. For other foundation can no man lay than that is laid, which is Jesus Christ. 1 Corinthians 3:9-11

First, we must remember that the apostle Paul is writing this letter to one church, the church at Corinth. It is in regard to the church at Corinth that Paul says, "I have laid the foundation." Paul uses the past tense, "I have laid," in referring to Corinth, when it is obvious that other church foundations were still to be laid by other apostles and prophets. This basically tells us that every local church needs to have a foundation laid.

The same is true in the natural world, every house needs a foundation. Jesus uses this analogy in Luke 6:47-49:

Whosoever cometh to Me, and heareth My sayings, and doeth them, I will shew you to whom he is like: he is like a man which built an house, and digged deep, and laid the foundation on a rock: and when the flood arose, the stream beat vehemently upon that house, and could not shake it: for it was founded upon a rock. But he that heareth, and doeth not, is like a man that without a foundation built an house upon the earth; against which the stream did beat vehemently, and immediately it fell; and the ruin of that house was great.

The Foundation of the Church

Jesus implied here that the builder of each house should be careful how he builds and that a foundation should be laid.

Much confusion exists in the body of Christ because we have not properly applied the Scriptures that refer to the Church universal, the entire Body of Christ, and those that refer to the church local (such as the second and third chapters of the Book of Revelation).

Now, let's answer our question, "Has the foundation of the Church already been laid?" The answer is twofold. Yes, the foundation of the Church universal has been laid with regard to the Word of God, not only the first principles of the doctrine of Christ (Heb. 5:12-6:2), but the entire doctrine of Christ as set forth in the New Testament. There are no new teachings. (Note: The foundational teachings of the church ended with the completion of God's holy Word and not with the death of the twelve apostles or the other apostles mentioned in the Scriptures.)

Speaking of the local church, I would say no, the foundation of most churches has not been laid. The fact that the principles are available in the Word of God does not imply that in fact every local church is founded on these same principles. I refer again to First Corinthians 3:9-11.

With the rapid spread of the gospel through Russia and other parts of the world, many new churches are being established, all of which need a foundation. As we look more intently into how the foundation of a church is to be laid, you will see more clearly why every local church must have a foundation.

How Is the Foundation of a Church to Be Laid?

You may have casually entered into reading this book believing the foundation of the Church has been laid. After reading the previous section, however, you may be thinking that every new local church must have a foundation laid and that many churches, for that matter many denominations, established in past years very possibly have no foundation at all. If this is true, many local churches stand on shaky ground.

Thus, we need to ask ourselves, "How is the foundation of a church to be laid?" I have found this a most intriguing question. At this point I would like to be honest with you and state that I do not have an exact answer. However, I believe the Lord is continuing to build His Church and is revealing from the Word of God through His servants, apostles and prophets truths that are bringing the Body of Christ closer to perfection. We Christians need to be open-minded in these last days and hunger for the truth.

The Foundation of the Church

For all who are reading this—pastors, laymen, teachers, evangelists, prophets or apostles—the significance of this question is that the integrity of every local church rests on the foundation. If many of the churches today have improper foundations or have no foundation at all, the Church as a whole has a big problem. All of the discipling programs, all the ministries and every other work of the Church will rest on a faulty or no foundation. This is why I believe the Church today has *no power*. With doors open for the gospel in countries such as Russia, it is not enough to preach the gospel and see souls saved and then let just anyone come in and start a church. A foundation must be laid first. A foundation must be laid for every local church, so that the church will still be standing for the next generation, strong and powerful, growing and bearing fruit.

There are two important passages of Scripture that will give us a clearer picture on laying the foundation:

Now therefore ye are no more strangers and foreigners, but fellowcitizens with the saints, and of the household of God; and are built upon the foundation of the apostles and prophets, Jesus Christ Himself being the chief corner stone; in whom all the building fitly framed together groweth unto an holy temple in the Lord: in whom ye also are builded together for an habitation of God through the Spirit. Ephesians 2:19-22

Now ye are the body of Christ, and members in particular. And God hath set some in the church, first apostles, secondarily prophets, thirdly teachers, after that miracles, then gifts of healings, helps, governments, diversities of tongues. 1 Corinthians 12:27-28

We can see a little more clearly from these passages how God's household is to be built. The first Scripture definitely links the laying of the foundation of a church to the work of the apostles and prophets. Interestingly, there is no Scripture that indicates others such as pastors, teachers or evangelists laid a foundation for a church.

Our second passage, from First Corinthians, also identifies the work of the apostles and prophets in laying the foundation in a church according to the divine order set up by God. Apostles were not only first, but also of first importance; the prophets were second and of secondary importance. Our God is a God of order and, beyond a doubt, God conveys the importance of the apostle and prophet here.

Note that governments is listed toward the end. The appointment of the local church government—elders (pastors) over the local body—would come some time later. But today pastors are sent out to start a church in another section of the city or in a neighboring town. This is not the way the Lord wants His Church to be built.

The Foundation of the Church

This is all very fine, but does the Book of Acts support building the foundation of the local church through apostles and prophets? We have a classic example in the establishment of the church at Antioch, as recorded in Acts 11:19-26.

> *Now they which were scattered abroad upon the persecution that arose about Stephen travelled as far as Phenice, and Cyprus, and Antioch, preaching the word to none but unto the Jews only. And some of them were men of Cyprus and Cyrene, which, when they were come to Antioch, spake unto the Grecians, preaching the Lord Jesus. And the hand of the Lord was with them: and a great number believed, and turned unto the Lord. Then tidings of these things came unto the ears of the church which was in Jerusalem: and they sent forth Barnabas, that he should go as far as Antioch. Who, when he came, and had seen the grace of God, was glad, and exhorted them all, that with purpose of heart they would cleave unto the Lord. For he was a good man, and full of the Holy Ghost and of faith: and much people was added unto the Lord. Then departed Barnabas to Tarsus, for to seek Saul: and when he had found him, he brought him unto Antioch. And it came to pass, that a whole year they assembled themselves with the church, and*

taught much people. And the disciples were called Christians first at Antioch.

Ah, my brethren in the Lord, if only this were the case today. A great move of God was begun by some unknown men. The Word does not give these men a name or title, saying only that a great number believed. You see, God was delighted to use anyone—evangelist or layman—in the preaching of the gospel. But once there was an assembly of believers, the Lord sent His apostles, Barnabas and Paul, to continue the preaching of the good news and to teach the converts. Barnabas and Paul labored for a year in Antioch, laying the foundation of the church and making disciples. God did not entrust the believers at Antioch to those who first preached there, but to His apostles and prophets.

Today as the Word of God spreads throughout the world, into South America, Africa, Russia and China and into the inner cities of America, it is not enough to sit back and pat ourselves on the back as many new believers are added. The local church needs to be established on a foundation which apostles and prophets have been called to lay.

Brothers and sisters in the Lord, this is God's way. Christ appointed apostles and prophets for the task of laying the foundation of the local church. He gifted these men so that a true and solid foundation could be laid upon Christ. Yes, it does make a difference. We shall soon see a great work of the Lord as Jesus builds His Church according to the pattern in the Word of God.

4

The Fivefold Ministry

My hope is that this book will help to revive the church's belief in the ministries of apostle and prophet. Do you believe that Jesus the carpenter knew how to build His Church? To eliminate Jesus' carefully laid out plans for building the Church is to build a church that will soon decay and crumble. Not only are local churches crumbling, but denominations too have been whittled down by the enemy. Why? Because they have a faulty foundation. Remember, just like a skyscraper, the Church is supported by the foundation. Every aspect, every Christian, every ministry suffers from the lack of a correctly laid foundation.

God's plan was to build His Church using the gifts that He had given to man. These gifts were apostles, prophets, evangelists, pastors and teachers, which we refer to as the fivefold ministry.

Wherefore He saith, When He ascended up on high, He led captivity captive, and gave gifts unto men. (Now that He ascended, what is it but that He also descended first into the lower parts of the earth? He that descended is the same also that ascended up far above all heavens, that He might fill all things.) And He gave some, apostles; and some, prophets; and some, evangelists; and some, pastors and teachers; for the perfecting of the saints, for the work of the ministry, for the edifying of the body of Christ.... Ephesians 4:8-12

Most Christians, for that matter most pastors, truly do not understand the role of the fivefold ministry in the life of the Church. Therefore, why incorporate these offices, why pray that these people be raised up within the Church? But to deny the fivefold ministry is to deny Jesus' plan for establishing and building His Church.

Today we have churches organized according to man-made patterns and laid down upon the traditions of men. For example, consider the leadership requirements of our churches. Some denominations have limited our God by requiring certain credentials before one can become a pastor or preach from the pulpit. But consider for a moment two of Jesus' followers, namely, Peter and John. "Now when they saw the boldness of Peter and John, and perceived that they were unlearned and ignorant men, they marvelled; and they took knowledge of them, that they had been with Jesus" (Acts 4:13).

Peter and John did not have impressive credentials. Their strength and courage did not come from having attended a Bible college, rather from having been with Jesus. All too many Christians are looked upon as ignorant, just as Peter and John were looked upon by the Jewish leaders, because of a lack of formal Bible training. But our churches need to raise up leaders who have spent time with Jesus and who do the works of Jesus; they do not need a seminary graduate who does the works taught by the seminary.

My contention is that the Church today is tainted with corruption and often is not following the pattern that Christ established. The result is a Church with little life and power. The reason is the Church has been improperly built, from the foundation up, due to the lack of the fivefold ministry.

The Purpose of the Fivefold Ministry

The passage of Scripture that the apostle Paul wrote in Ephesians 4:8-12 is tremendous. There is so

A Church of Power Is Emerging

much in this passage that it is worth further study to learn both the purpose and function of the fivefold ministry and what the Lord intended the Church to become when He gave these gifted people to the Body.

First, we ask ourselves, "What is the purpose of the fivefold ministry?" Our answer lies in verse 12 "for the perfecting of the saints, for the work of the ministry, for the edifying of the body of Christ...." It may be helpful to also read this from the New International Version, "to prepare God's people for works of service, so that the body of Christ may be built up...."

The purpose is "so that the body of Christ may be built up." Jesus had already stated in Matthew 16, "...I will build My Church...." Jesus is carrying through on His promise to build the Church by giving the fivefold ministry gifts to the Body of Christ. As we have already learned, the foundation of the Church is laid by the apostles and prophets. Part of their gifting is to dig the foundation deep and lay it upon Jesus Christ.

Brothers and sisters in the Lord, we assume that because our leaders talk about Jesus the foundation has been properly laid upon Jesus. This is not necessarily true. Brethren, a foundation laid by a pastor will be different from that laid by an apostle and prophet. Why? Because, as we shall see later, the grace of our Lord has gifted the apostle for this work. Only when the Lord has re-established these gifted people in the Church and we have a Church that has been properly built up on a sound foundation will we be able to say, "This is how the Lord intended the Church to be built." That time is coming soon.

The second question we should ask concerning the fivefold ministry is "What is the function of these gifted people? How exactly is the Church to be built up?" Returning to verse 12, we will have our answer, "for the perfecting of the saints, for the work of the ministry...." To disciple a newborn Christian is to take him or her from the point of conversion to perfection, to the point where they are ready to do the works of service. This is a never-ending process, as new converts continually pour into the local body.

One of the facts one might overlook in the life of Jesus was His equipping of His followers. When we study the Scriptures we learn that Jesus was called an apostle, a prophet, a shepherd and a teacher. Surely He also was an evangelist, even though the Scripture does not specifically say this. So we see all the giftings of the fivefold ministry within Christ. With these giftings our Lord trained the 12 disciples. We would be naive to believe all the same giftings are

A Church of Power Is Emerging

no longer needed today in equipping the saints. But, in fact, when Jesus ascended to be with the Father, He distributed these giftings among His followers (lest any man think he is like Christ). He distributed them by appointing some as apostles, some as prophets, some as evangelists and some as shepherds and teachers.

These gifted people were an extension of Jesus Christ Himself for continuing the preparation of God's people for works of service. They are vital to the building up of the Body of Christ. God's grace is upon them. They are to equip and train disciples as Jesus did. For what? For the work of the ministry.

Jesus said, "I must work the works of Him that sent Me..." (Jn. 9:4). Likewise, for us the work of the ministry is to do the works of Him who sent us, Jesus Christ. Jesus' works of ministry were to preach the gospel, to heal the sick, the lame and the blind, to cast out demons, to raise the dead and also to make disciples to carry out His work. This is the work of the ministry.

The third and last question we are going to ask in regard to the fivefold ministry is "What did the Lord intend the Church to become?" The answer very simply is a mature Church or a Church coming to the fullness of Christ. We need to continue reading the passage from Ephesians 4:

The Fivefold Ministry

And He gave some, apostles; and some, prophets; and some, evangelists; and some, pastors and teachers; for the perfecting of the saints, for the work of the ministry, for the edifying of the body of Christ: till we all come in the unity of the faith, and of the knowledge of the Son of God, unto a perfect man, unto the measure of the stature of the fulness of Christ: that we henceforth be no more children, tossed to and fro, and carried about with every wind of doctrine, by the sleight of men, and cunning craftiness, whereby they lie in wait to deceive; but speaking the truth in love, may grow up into Him in all things, which is the head, even Christ: from whom the whole body fitly joined together and compacted by that which every joint supplieth, according to the effectual working in the measure of every part, maketh increase of the body unto the edifying of itself in love (vv. 11-16).

The Lord wants to bring each individual into maturity, but more so His collective Body. The Lord wants to perfect His saints until we come "unto the measure of the stature of the fullness of Christ." The operation of the fivefold ministry in the Church will bring unity to the brethren in faith and in the knowledge of the Son of God, as each believer matures as a disciple and functions with the gift(s) Christ has given him. This leads to perfection and to the fullness of Christ, which is where all of us want to be.

A Church of Power Is Emerging

Now listen very carefully. If your local church has not the functioning of apostle, prophet, evangelist, pastor and teacher, then your local body will never be built up properly. It will *never* come into unity in the faith and in the knowledge of the Son of God. Your church will be unbalanced, lopsided, crippled. Your church will be immature, your members immature—mere infants, and you will be immature. You and your church will be tossed to and fro, trying a little of this and a little of that, this program and then that program, this scheme and then another scheme. You'll be approached by outsiders, and by their cunningness and craftiness you will be deceived and led astray, off the mark, off the work that Christ intended for you. You will have a view toward a system of error.

Christ instituted and called out apostles and prophets to establish and lay the foundation of a church, not pastors and teachers. Christ instituted the fivefold ministry, not one or two men, to build the church and equip the saints. If God's people ever want to see the power of God manifest today, then we must go back to the Master's plan for building the Church.

Right now the Lord is raising up apostles and prophets. They are very distinctly set apart because of the anointing on their life. Yet the established Church, the leadership in church bodies, is rejecting these men. Jesus will continue to build His Church and very soon will call forth His remnant to come out, and be separated and establish a new work. Be ready!

The Fullness Versus Revival

Revival is a term with which we and even the unsaved are familiar. We talk about revival, preach on revival, pray for revival and long to see revival come. There are many books written on the various revivals. We read about them and are amazed at the work of God. We study these books, searching for key ingredients so that we too may experience revival in our local churches and cities.

First, let's look at the meaning of the word *revive*. *Vine's Expository Dictionary* defines it as "to live again," "to regain life." Webster's dictionary defines it as "to come back to consciousness," "to recover strength, vigor, spirits, etc." You get the idea, don't you?

Throughout the Old Testament we see the people of Israel turn away from their God and indulge in sin and corruption. They forsook the ways of the Lord. God's wrath arose and judgment came upon the people, bringing famine, plagues, and enemies who besieged them. They then turned back to God, in order that God would revive them. Psalm 85:6 says, "Wilt Thou not revive us again: that Thy people may rejoice in Thee?" God was faithful to revive His people and restore the nation.

Now what about the word revival and how it pertains to the Church in New Testament times? This writer is of the opinion that the Church today is in error, in sin, and has missed the mark and that there are many Christians sitting in the church pews who like the Israelites, have taken on the sins of the people around them. They have become worldly in many respects.

Jesus said to the church at Sardis: "I know your deeds; you have a reputation of being alive, but you are dead. Wake up! Strengthen what remains and is about to die, for I have not found your deeds complete in the sight of My God" (Rev. 3:1b-2, NIV). This church at Sardis needed revival. The believers needed to repent as the Lord commanded, so they would "come back to life."

Yes, in a sense, revival needs to come to local bodies and to the Church as a whole. Yes, the Church needs to come back to life. *But*, here is where we need to pause for a moment. If we were to examine many of the "revivals" that have occurred, we might find that the churches in which these revivals took place have grown cold and have turned back to their old ways. You see, revival only brings us back to the point at which we were prior to falling into sin. If there had been a system of error set up within the local church, or even in the denomination, then revival would bring back life,

The Fivefold Ministry

but into a sinful environment that soon will put out the flames of the revival. Is revival really what the Church should be looking for?

The answer is in the Word of God. The New Testament never speaks of revival. We, the Body of Christ, are to come "unto the measure of the stature of the fulness of Christ" (Eph. 4:13).

We, the Church, are the "fulness of Christ" as written in Ephesians 1:22-23. This statement indicates the position of the Church, much as we are the "righteousness of Christ." I believe the fulness is positional because of the fivefold ministry, whereby gifted people are to bring us unto the fullness, as we discussed in the previous section.

Our vision for the Church, our desire for the Church, should be for her to come unto the measure of the stature of the fulness of Christ, not revival. We want revival because we think of exciting meetings, singing, repentance, flowing of charismatic gifts, signs and wonders. There's nothing wrong with these things, but the Lord wants us to come into maturity. Repentance must lead to obedience to His Word, not back to a system of error. Our Father in Heaven desires His children to come "unto the measure of the *stature* of the fulness of Christ." *Stature* means "height," unto the height of Christ. We are not speaking of the physical capabilities of

Jesus, but of His spiritual capability in *all* respects. This includes the love that Christ had, "...love one another; as I have loved you...." It includes His mercy and compassion and the desire for the lost to be saved. It includes His preaching and all the power of the Holy Spirit to heal and cast out demons. It includes His unity with the Father and Holy Spirit, so that we too would be one.

Brothers and sisters in the Lord, I commend to you a better way, to the fullness of our Lord Jesus Christ.

5

The Apostle

Are Apostles for Today?

Most Christians do not believe that the apostolic ministry exists today. For generations Christians have been taught a variety of views, all of which basically deny the existence of apostles today. There are those who have been taught that there were only 13 apostles, Paul being the 13th, and that this is where the line ended. Another teaching is that by the end of the writing of the Scriptures, the foundation of the Church had already been laid, and therefore there is no longer a need for apostles to lay a foundation. Christ as the foundation has already been laid, and it is sufficient for pastors who can aptly apply the Word of God to begin new churches.

Are both of these concepts in error scripturally?

Only in recent years has the concept of the fivefold ministry surfaced. As Christians have had the opportunity of reading the bible and studying it, they have discovered the passage in Ephesians 4 at which we have been looking. Clearly, our Lord's appointing of those gifted for the fivefold ministry after His ascension indicates that these men were to operate in their respective offices after the ascension of Christ. Today, I see pastors and teachers, and I know of some evangelists and even some who claim to be prophets, but where are the apostles? "Are apostles for today?" the student inquires.

First, I would like to say that we do not walk by sight. The fact that we do not see many so-called apostles in the Church today does not mean they do not exist. We walk by faith and should believe the Word of God. The Word of God should be our final authority and what we put our trust in. Amen!

Let us look at the progression of apostolic ministry in the Bible. If, in fact, there were others aside from the 13 raised up by our Lord who were referred to as apostles, it would indicate that the Lord intended this ministry to continue. We will consider two others in the Scriptures as apostles of the Lord, Barnabas and Timothy.

Of Barnabas we read,

But the Jews stirred up the devout and honorable women, and the chief men of the city, and raised persecution against Paul and Barnabas, and expelled them out of their coasts. But they shook off the dust of their feet against them, and came unto Iconium. And the disciples were filled with joy, and with the Holy Ghost. And it came to pass in Iconium, that they went both together into the synagogue of the Jews, and so spake, that a great multitude both of the Jews and also of the Greeks believed. But the unbelieving Jews stirred up the Gentiles, and made their minds evil affected against the brethren. Long time therefore abode they speaking boldly in the Lord, which gave testimony unto the word of His grace, and granted signs and wonders to be done by their hands. But the multitude of the city was divided: and part held with the Jews, and part with the apostles. Acts 13:50–14:4

Which when the apostles, Barnabas and Paul, heard of, they rent their clothes, and ran in among the people, crying out.... Acts 14:14

The first three verses are included to point out that this passage is referring to Paul and Barnabas, that in Iconium both Paul and Barnabas spoke the Word of the Lord and also did signs and wonders, the works of an apostle. Verses 4 and 14 clearly indicate that Barnabas was an apostle.

Of Timothy it is written,

Then came he to Derbe and Lystra: and, behold, a certain disciple was there, named Timotheus, the son of a certain woman, which was a Jewess, and believed; but his father was a Greek: which was well reported of by the brethren that were at Lystra and Iconium. Him would Paul have to go forth with him; and took and circumcised him because of the Jews which were in those quarters: for they knew all that his father was a Greek. Acts 16:1-3

Here Timothy, a believer of high report, is asked to join the apostle Paul on his missionary journey.

For this cause have I sent unto you Timotheus, who is my beloved son, and faithful in the Lord, who shall bring you into remembrance of my ways which be in Christ, as I teach every where in every church. 1 Corinthians 4:17

In this passage we see the spiritual growth of Timothy. Paul sent Timothy to Corinth to remind them of the teachings of Christ. Timothy had been a faithful disciple of Paul and had learned well the teachings of Jesus.

Paul, and Silvanus, and Timotheus, unto the church of the Thessalonians which is in God the Father and in the Lord Jesus Christ.... 1 Thessalonians 1:1

The Apostle

Nor of men sought we glory, neither of you, nor yet of others, when we might have been burdensome, as the apostles of Christ. 1 Thessalonians 2:6

Paul wrote his letter to the Thessalonians on behalf of himself, Silvanus and Timothy, all of whom he refers to as apostles of Christ (v. 6). This seems to indicate more than just an association of Timothy with the apostle Paul, rather in fact that Timothy himself was an apostle. The whole point here is that we see the Lord raising up another apostle to use, namely, Timothy. The same was true of Barnabas and even Silvanus.

It is clear from the Scriptures which we have just read that the apostolic ministry did not end with the Twelve nor with Paul, but it continued on throughout the New Testament. Does it still continue in the 20th century?

Let us reason for a minute. We see in the Church today pastors and teachers and evangelists. Even prophets have been recognized in many church circles. Therefore, we see four of the five gifts mentioned in Ephesians 4 in operation. Would it not seem reasonable to believe that if Christ intended four of the fivefold ministry gifts to be utilized today, that He intended all five gifts to be used? Ephesians 4:11-13 is a powerful passage supporting the role of apostles and prophets in the Church. Never do we see in the Scriptures these gifts revoked by our Lord.

A Church of Power Is Emerging

In the next sections as we study what an apostle is and the function of an apostle, we will come to understand the specific gifting that the apostle has and the need for such gifting in the building up of the Body of Christ. Let me give a little example for you to think about.

If we could build houses today that needed no plumbing, then we could say, "We do not need a plumber in the building of this house." But, of course, we do need plumbing facilities. Someone might then suggest, "Let the carpenter read the plumber's handbook and practice for a time, then he could do the work of the plumber as well." Yes, this might work well in the natural world, and it could save a lot of money. The catch is when we apply this to the spiritual building of the Church, we see that it is Jesus who gives out the gifts. This means that no matter how smart he is or how much the pastor, teacher, evangelist or prophet reads God's manual, there will never be a replacement for the God-given gift of apostle.

Many churches look at themselves and see a large, growing, lively, scripturally based church and assume that they have a sound foundation. Beloved, you are mistaken. The devil has fooled you. To put it simply, if the apostolic ministry was ignored in the establishment of a particular local church, the foundation has not been properly laid. Furthermore, the whole Church is suffering because of it.

Let us now look into the ministry of an apostle.

An Apostle Is a Messenger

Apostle, from the Greek work *Apostolos*, means "a messenger" or "one who is sent." Jesus was an apostle, as we learn from Hebrews 3:1, "Wherefore, holy brethren, partakes of the heavenly calling, consider the apostle and High Priest of our profession, Christ Jesus...." Jesus was sent forth by the Father with a specific message of salvation to a lost world. Jesus extended this apostolic ministry when He chose the Twelve. It is interesting to note that Jesus did *not* choose 12 pastors, nor 12 teachers, nor 12 evangelists, nor even 12 prophets to send forth. He chose 12 disciples and designated them as apostles because the message needed to *go forth*.

I believe that as long as the message needs to go forth, overseas and locally to our inner cities and suburbs and outlying towns, there will still be a need for apostles. Even in the Book of Revelation there is mention of apostles and prophets. They were sent to the city of Babylon, "Babylon, the great, the mother of harlots and abomination of the earth" (Rev. 17:5). In one hour the city was made desolate, destroyed. Then we have this Scripture recorded, "Rejoice over her, thou heaven, and ye holy apostles and prophets; for God hath avenged you on her" (Rev. 18:20). Yes, as long as the message of salvation needs to go forth there always will be apostles.

The first priority of an apostle therefore is to act as a messenger. But what exactly is the message to be proclaimed? Here lies the heart of the difference between a true apostle and a false apostle.

Therefore if any man be in Christ, he is a new creature: old things are passed away; behold, all things are become new. And all things are of God, who hath reconciled us to Himself by Jesus Christ, and hath given to us the ministry of reconciliation; to wit, that God was in Christ, reconciling the world unto Himself, not imputing their trespasses unto them; and hath committed unto us the word of reconciliation. Now then we are ambassadors for Christ, as though God did beseech you by us: we pray you in Christ's stead, be ye reconciled to God. For He hath made him to be sin for us, who knew no sin; that we might be made the righteousness of God in Him. 2 Corinthians 5:17-21

The message of a true apostle is the reconciliation of man unto God through Jesus Christ. Paul fine tuned this message in First Corinthians 15:1-4,

The Apostle

Moreover, brethren, I declare unto you the gospel which I preached unto you, which also ye have received, and wherein ye stand; by which also ye are saved, if ye keep in memory what I preached unto you, unless ye have believed in vain. For I delivered unto you first of all that which I also received, how that Christ died for our sins according to the scriptures; and that He was buried, and that He rose again the third day according to the scriptures....

Of first importance in the message of the apostle Paul was the death and resurrection of Jesus Christ. Here lies the heart of the apostolic ministry. There are many claiming to be apostles, who preach a different message of salvation other than the death and resurrection of Jesus Christ. They are all false apostles. There are Christians who go forth throughout the world with different words and different teachings on many subjects. They are not apostles. They may be teachers, but they are not apostles. There are Christian leaders who have established new churches, but unless the message of the cross and resurrection was preached, with the subsequent conversion of new souls, unless the foundation of the local church was laid, then these men were not apostles. They simply began a new church with other Christians. This kind of thing is going on today.

If you believe that the Lord has called you to be an apostle, then a simple test with which to begin is whether this message of reconciliation has been seared into your heart. Has it?

An Apostle Lays the Foundation

Before we continue our study of apostles, specifically their function in laying the foundation of the local churches, it would help if we had a broader understanding of the role of the Church in relationship to the Kingdom of God. Jesus preached and taught much concerning the Kingdom of God or The kingdom of Heaven, (synonymous terms). This was an important concept to our Lord, which we should not overlook.

The Relationship of the Church to the Kingdom of God

The word *kingdom* can be considered as two words: *King's domain*. It is the territory over which the King rules. The Kingdom of God then is the extension of God's rule to the uttermost parts of the universe, including all within it: angels, creatures and mankind.

With the fall of satan and then the fall of man, other kingdoms came into existence, which all were under the influence of satan. We see this in Matthew

4:8-9, where the devil tempts our Lord in the wilderness by offering him all the kingdoms of the world if He would fall down and worship him. Ephesians 2:2 refers to satan as the ruler of the air. The earth was a mess when our Lord came 2,000 years ago.

Then, our Lord came preaching this message: "The time is fulfilled, and the kingdom of God is at hand: repent ye, and believe the gospel" (Mk. 1:15). The time had come when satan and his influence and rule over the kingdoms of the earth would be confronted and the Kingdom of God would be advanced. The instrument through which God's Kingdom was to be advanced was the Church. The Church would be composed of "God's elect," or "God's called-out and assembled people."

The relationship between the Church and the Kingdom of God is established in this passage:

And Jesus answered and said unto him, Blessed art thou, Simon Bar-jona: for flesh and blood hath not revealed it unto thee, but My Father which is in heaven. And I say also unto thee, That thou art Peter, and upon this rock I will build My church; and the gates of hell shall not prevail against it. And I will give unto thee the keys of the kingdom of heaven: and whatsoever thou shalt bind on earth shall be bound in heaven: and whatsoever thou shalt loose on earth shall be loosed in heaven. Matthew 16:17-19

Here for the first time Jesus declared He would build His Church, and it would be to the Church that keys to the Kingdom of Heaven would be given. Keys represent the authority or power to open or close doors. This authority and power given to the Church was one of binding and loosing. The relationship of the Church to the Kingdom of God then is that the Church has now become the instrument on earth through which our Lord has chosen to advance His Kingdom. It will be to the body of believers who make up the Church that power and authority will be given to bind the strong man, the devil, and to loose those whom satan has bound.

From this passage we can plainly see the broader picture of the main work of the Church, that is, to advance the Kingdom of God. It is obvious from the words, "and the gates of hell shall not prevail against it," that there would be a long battle ahead for the Church and that the Church was intended to be not only a militant Church but also a victorious Church. Jesus portrayed the same picture in this Scripture also: "And from the days of John the Baptist unto now the kingdom of heaven suffereth violence, and the violent take it by force" (Mt. 11:12).

To be violent and forceful is one thing, but to be victorious is something else. Do you belong to a victorious church? (I'm referring to your local church.)

Why do you say you belong to a victorious church? Think about it for a moment. Armies do not just get lucky and win battles. The armies which are properly assembled and well equipped and which have a good strategic plan are the ones that are victorious. When the United Nations fought Iraq over Kuwait, the United Nations won a great victory because they were properly assembled, well equipped and had a good plan of attack. In order for a church to be victorious, it too must be properly built up, properly assembled, with each Christian equipped for battle. A church should not take its battle with the devil lightly, and we should not take the building up of a church lightly either. It begins with the laying of the foundation. Let's do it according to the Word of God.

Remember, Jesus is coming back for a glorious and victorious Church, and *soon*.

Laying the Foundation

To begin this section I would like us to recall this Scripture: "Except the Lord build the house, they labour in vain that build it..." (Ps. 127:1).

How many pastors and church leaders quote this Scripture over and over again, yet truly do not understand its meaning and consequences. If my job were to be involved with the building up of a local body, then this Scripture would cause me to seek the way Jesus intended a church to be built. Otherwise all my work could be, *no, would be*, in vain. Amen! "Have I labored all my life to build this church in vain?" This thought could bring a few chills down the spines of some who are reading this. What is the way Jesus has chosen to build a church?

These two passages will help us greatly.

For we are labourers together with God: ye are God's husbandry, ye are God's building. According to the grace of God which is given unto me, as a wise masterbuilder, I have laid the foundation, and another buildeth thereon. But let every man take heed how he buildeth thereupon. For other foundation can no man lay than that is laid, which is Jesus Christ. 1 Corinthians 3:9-11

Now ye are the body of Christ, and members in particular. And God hath set some in the church, first apostles, secondarily prophets, thirdly teachers, after that miracles, then gifts of healings, helps, governments, diversities of tongues. 1 Corinthians 12:27-28

When the apostle Paul preached the gospel in different towns and cities, where the gospel was received, Paul would stay to start a church. From the first passage above we gather that Paul would lay a foundation for the church, and others later would build thereupon. Laying the foundation was a separate undertaking. We need to recognize that fact.

The Apostle

Our second passage indicates that God had some divine order in the Body of Christ, that, in fact, apostles were to be first and prophets second. (Note: Pastors are not mentioned in this verse. I do not say this to demean or degrade this gifted ministry, but so that we do not build a faulty foundation.) The ministry of the apostle comes first in laying the foundation of the local church. He builds together with the prophet, as we saw in Ephesians 2:19-22: "The household of God [is] built upon the foundation of the apostles and prophets...." Yes, our Lord Jesus Christ is the builder, and it is He who has chosen these men.

Two obvious questions then are "Why are apostles first in laying the foundation?" and "Why can't pastors or teachers lay a foundation?" The heart of the answer is seen in our passage on the fivefold ministry from Ephesians 4:

But unto every one of us is given grace according to the measure of the gift of Christ. Wherefore He saith, When He ascended up on high, He led captivity captive, and gave gifts unto men (vv. 7-8).

This refers to the gifting of some as apostles, prophets, etc.

Jesus is the One who builds a church. He has a divine pattern set in Heaven, which should be followed specifically. The building of a church begins with the laying of the foundation, as we have seen. This is a very important task upon which the integrity of the whole building will rest, and most important is the fact that Jesus Christ Himself is the Chief Cornerstone. Christ has chosen to gift but a few to lay the foundation. Christ has specifically told us in His Word that the work of laying the foundation starts with the apostle. What sets the apostle apart is the measure of God's grace given unto him to accomplish this task. Paul said, "According to the grace of God which is given unto me, as a wise masterbuilder, I have laid the foundation, and another buildeth thereon" (1 Cor. 3:10). Paul was able to lay the foundation of the church in a unique and powerful way because he was a wise masterbuilder, and Paul attributed this ability simply to the grace of God.

Now, you might wonder exactly what is a masterbuilder. What sets him apart from those with seemingly similar gifts. The answer is *revelation knowledge*.

The apostle Paul wrote,

How that by revelation He made known unto me the mystery; (as I wrote afore in few words, whereby when ye read, ye may understand my knowledge in the mystery of Christ) which in other ages was not made known unto the sons of men, as it is now revealed unto His holy apostles and prophets by the Spirit.... Ephesians 3:3-5

Paul said it was by revelation that he received knowledge in the mystery of Christ. God reveals mysteries to His holy apostles and prophets through the Holy Spirit. To somewhat understand this we can go to Galatians 1:15-17,

But when it pleased God, who separated me from my mother's womb, and called me by His grace, to reveal His Son in me, that I might preach Him among the heathen; immediately I conferred not with flesh and blood: neither went I up to Jerusalem to them which were apostles before me; but I went into Arabia, and returned again unto Damascus.

Here lies a great example of revelation knowledge. Upon his conversion on the road to Damascus, Paul conferred not with man (flesh and blood), nor did he go to the established apostles in Jerusalem to learn the mysteries of Christ. Paul received his knowledge directly from the Lord. Listen very carefully. Paul was a leader among the Jews prior to his conversion and was well learned in the Old Testament, but it was by revelation that he learned of the mysteries of Christ. Similarly, today those whom the Lord has called and gifted as apostles and prophets will be set apart by their receiving knowledge of the mysteries of Jesus Christ directly from our Lord. They will not attribute their knowledge and understanding of the Word of God, specifically that which pertains to our Lord, to any man, any scholar, any seminary or Bible college, rather to divine revelation by the grace of God. This revelation knowledge will be apparent to others, for like our Lord, they will teach and preach as one with authority.

> *And when James, Cephas, and John, who seemed to be pillars, perceived the grace that was given unto me, they gave to me and Barnabas the right hands of fellowship; that we should go unto the heathen, and they unto the circumcision.* Galatians 2:9

This Scripture indicates how apostles and prophets and gifted men of God should be received by the Body of Christ. Others will perceive the grace of God upon them and the revelation knowledge received of our Lord, and thus they should accept them and listen to them. It was not because of credentials nor degrees that these men were accepted, but because of the authoritative word that they spoke.

Another simple example of this was the apostle Peter, when Jesus asked the disciples, "But whom say ye that I am? And Simon Peter answered and said, Thou art the Christ, the Son of the living God."

Jesus replied, "Blessed art thou, Simon Bar-jona: for flesh and blood hath not revealed it unto thee, but My Father which is in heaven" (Mt. 16:15-17). It was by divine revelation that Peter knew Jesus was the Christ.

Most of us will be trained and equipped in the Word of God and in the works of Christ by others. Jesus was the Master; He Himself taught the disciples. The point of all this is that God sets *some* aside to whom He reveals Himself and His ways, according to the task at hand. One task is the laying of the foundation of the Church. We definitely need God's chosen apostles to help us build local churches in this day and age. God's plan has not changed.

If the Church is to be built on Christ, then those whom the Lord has chosen to lay foundations should be fixed on Jesus. We should have it no other way. Paul was a prime example. "For I determined not to know any thing among you, save Jesus Christ, and Him crucified" (1 Cor. 2:2). From this Scripture you get a clear picture of the apostle Paul fixed on Jesus. How beautiful. Paul was determined to focus on Christ and the work of the cross no matter where he was, and this is attributed to revelation knowledge and the grace of God. This is a sign of an apostle, he is set on the Lord.

Most Christians today will say, "I know Jesus Christ. Our church preaches Jesus Christ and Him crucified." That is true to some degree. The problem, however, lies with the fact the Christians in the local church are also familiar with the world and its ways. Christians today know all about sporting events—the outcome of last Sunday's football games, who will be in the playoffs for the World Series, and so forth; they talk about the latest movies and home videos; they know where to dine during the week; they know how to spend their money on worldly things and, of course, how to have a good time. We can go on and on. This is why the Body of Christ is lukewarm, the Church has diluted the ways of the Lord with the ways of the people around them.

We need apostles in the Church who will speak out against the sinful ways of the world, who will say to the disciples, "Know nothing save Jesus Christ and Him crucified."

For this cause have I sent unto you Timotheous, who is my beloved son, and faithful in the Lord, who shall bring you into remembrance of my ways which be in Christ, as I teach every where in every church. 1 Corinthians 4:17

This passage affirms that what was important in everything that Paul taught was that his ways were in Christ. Paul did not waiver in his teaching, but taught the same things in every local church that he founded or visited.

The Apostle

The point that I'm trying to make here is how much an apostle is set on Christ. This *must* be the case in laying a sure foundation in the local body.

I said at the beginning of this book that a Church of power is emerging. By revelation, I have seen the importance of simple truths in the Word of God as they relate to the Lord's task at hand and that the preponderance of truth revolves around the basic teachings of Christ and the work of the cross.

Are we missing it today? Have we been seduced by the devil into focusing on all kinds of strange teachings and doctrines, or have we even by focusing on the Holy Spirit and gifts and such taken our eyes off the Lord? "Let us fix our eyes on Jesus, the author and perfecter of our faith..." (Heb. 12:2, NIV).

We need apostles today to re-establish the teachings of Christ in the Church.

An Apostle Perfects the Saints

So far we have looked at two functions of the apostle. The primary function of an apostle is to be a messenger, to proclaim the message of reconciliation of man to God through Jesus Christ. The second function, somewhat in order, would be to lay the foundation of the local church. This foundation would be laid upon Jesus Christ—the teachings of Christ, the works of Christ, the commands of Christ, the cross, the resurrection and the return of our Lord. This the apostle would do with a special gifting by the grace of God.

Yes, in the Word of God we have all of the doctrines of Jesus Christ. Yes, anyone could attempt to lay a foundation through gathering all this knowledge. A lay person, a pastor, a teacher or an evangelist could endeavor to start a church. But what we have learned is that apostles (and prophets) teach by revelation knowledge. They do not teach new knowledge, but revealed truths in the Word of God which come alive to accomplish the task the Lord has given to them.

Remember this Scripture?

Now ye are the body of Christ, and members in particular. And God hath set some in the church, first apostles, secondarily prophets, thirdly teachers, after that miracles, then gifts of healings, helps, governments, diversities of tongues. Are all apostles? are all prophets? are all teachers? are all workers of miracles? 1 Corinthians 12:27-29

The answer to all of these questions is an emphatic, *no*. God has set *some* in the Church to be apostles. There are only some who will be in the fivefold ministry. There are too many Christians filling positions to which they have not been called and for which they have not been gifted.

The third function of an apostle that we want to study is the perfecting of the saints. We take this from our familiar Scripture on the fivefold ministry, Ephesians 4:11-13.

And He gave some, apostles; and some, prophets; and some, evangelists; and some, pastors and teachers; for the perfecting of the saints, for the work of the ministry, for the edifying of the body of Christ: till we all come in the unity of the faith, and of the knowledge of the Son of God, unto a perfect man, unto the measure of the stature of the fulness of Christ....

We cannot separate "the perfecting of the saints" from the remainder of the verse. The "perfecting of the saints" is for "the work of the ministry" so that the body of Christ will be edified. *Edified* means "built up." Furthermore, the goal is for the Church to come into unity, into perfection, unto the fullness of Christ. Quite a statement.

We make a big mistake when we do not consider "the work of the ministry" while trying to teach and train and equip the saints. We discussed previously that the work of ministry for all saints should be the works of Jesus Christ. Only then can the edifying of the Body of Christ come to pass. *Edify* is related to the word *edifice*, or building. Particularly, edifice means "an imposing building." When properly built, the Body of Christ should be an imposing spiritual force to be perceived as an unmovable pillar in the community which stands for righteousness and holiness and which wages war against the forces of evil.

The perfecting of the saints is a combined effort of the fivefold ministry, but I believe it is the apostle who should take the leading role as to how to perfect the saints. It is the apostle who will have the revelation of Christ and seek to make disciples after our Lord. As the apostle Paul says in First Corinthians 11:1 (NIV), "Follow my example, as I follow the example of Christ." It will also be the apostle who will build according to the Lord's plan and incorporate the fivefold ministry into the operation of every local church. As Christ had all the gifts of the fivefold ministry, it is important these gifts be extended in the Church today. The apostle, the prophet, the evangelist, the pastor and the teacher all have a specific and significant role in regard to building up the Body of Christ.

The apostle is given tremendous insight and wisdom into the making of true disciples. As we discussed previously, disciples will be equipped *for the work of the ministry*: to preach the gospel, to heal the sick, to cast out demons and to perform miracles, signs and wonders. Apostles will seek to make disciples as the Lord did, by hands-on training, by experience.

There are two aspects of perfecting the saints, of edifying the Body of Christ. One is the individual perfecting of every Christian, as we have already considered. The second aspect is perfecting the saints collectively in the functioning of the Church as a whole. The apostle Paul had great insight into the workings of the Body of Christ collectively, as seen from the following passage:

For as the body is one, and hath many members, and all the members of that one body, being many, are one body: so also is Christ. For by one Spirit are we all baptized into one body, whether we be Jews or Gentiles, whether we be bond or free; and have been all made to drink into one Spirit. For the body is not one member, but many. If the foot shall say, Because I am not the hand, I am not of the body; is it therefore not of the body? And if the ear shall say, Because I am not the eye, I am not of the body; is it therefore not of the body? If the whole body were an eye, where were the hearing? If the whole were hearing, where were the smelling? But now hath God set the members every one of them in the body, as it hath pleased Him. And if they were all one member, where were the body? But now are they many members, yet but one body. And the eye cannot say unto the hand, I have no need of thee: nor again the head to the feet, I have no need of

you. Nay, much more those members of the body, which seem to be more feeble, are necessary....
1 Corinthians 12:12-22

The picture Paul paints for us is that of a man, all of whose members fit together in a delicate and intricate way. Similarly, in the Word of God we have the picture of the Church as a building, erected upward from the foundation. The point here is we have a tendency to see the Church solely in an evangelistic way, as gathering in the lost, as a gathering of members or as a gathering of stones. It becomes "a numbers game."

Paul saw the Church differently. The Body of Christ was not a gathering of stones, but the building of stones. He saw the Church as an edifice, as a magnificent structure, as a habitation for the Lord and an instrument for furthering the Kingdom of God. It was a building wherein each member was gifted, each member was important, each member functioned as a rock that would be placed rock upon rock until the building was completed to perfection.

This is not the case today. For example, we do not see the operation of many spiritual gifts in the Body of Christ. "Now there are diversities of gifts, but the same Spirit" (1 Cor. 12:4). These gifts are the word of wisdom, the word of knowledge, faith, gifts of healing, working of miracles, prophecy, discerning of spirits, divers kinds of tongues and interpretation of tongues (see 1 Cor. 12:8-10). We also see gifts of helps and governments listed in First Corinthians 12:28, and there are others.

Do you know those in your local body with the gift of discernment? Is this gift used? How about the gift of faith? Is the working of miracles allowed to operate in your local body? Do all your people know who this person is? Why not? God knows there are those Christians who need a miracle. Let's not forget, our God is supernatural. He delights in doing miracles for His children. We can go on and on with all the gifts.

The problem is that in many circumstances the congregation will see the pastor or a preacher minister in the gifts, but that's it. The pastor is the one who preaches, evangelizes, hears from God, does the praying for the sick, prophesies, discerns, is the government, and on and on. It is no wonder many churches remain in infancy. All the gifts that God has given to the church members remain locked up, never to be discovered, and the church leaders wonder why there is criticism, unrest and talk of leaving among the brethren. This may be a slight exaggeration, but you get the picture.

What if God spoke to a church and said, "There is one million dollars somewhere in your sanctuary."

Would that church not tear up the entire building to find the money? Now, how much more valuable are the different gifts the Lord has given to each member? Those in the fivefold ministry, particularly the apostle, will have a desire to see these gifts manifested in the Body of Christ.

Because the Church has operated for such a long time without apostles and prophets, it is hard to conceive what a scriptural Church would be like. The Church has suffered greatly in every respect because of a faulty foundation. But it is with hope that I look to the near future when the true Church will emerge, a Church endued with power. Yes, the Lord is building this Church. Will you be a part of this move of God?

Other functions of an Apostle

We have touched on but a few of the many facets of an apostle. Let us continue in the direction of developing the local church. Following the preaching of the gospel, came the laying of a foundation. This was followed by perfecting of the saints for the works of ministry so that the Body of Christ would be built up.

Once a church could stand on its own, having been taught the doctrines and ways of Christ, the apostle's job was to go on and repeat the whole process in another city or town. Prior to leaving, the apostle had one last thing to be done, the institution of the church government. The church needed leaders now that the apostles or apostle and prophet were moving on. Who would be the leader(s) of this particular church? It would be the *elders* or *pastors*. The appointment of elders would complete the establishment of this local church, except for a few minor details. This appointment of elders is a very crucial and delicate matter which we will discuss under the topic of pastors and church government.

Another function of an apostle which is very evident in the Word of God is that of correction in the local church. Much of the New Testament writings concern correction. The Word of God, of course, should be our final authority, but God has vessels to implement certain tasks in the Body of Christ. All Christians can use the Word of God for correction; but for correction of the whole Body of Christ, the founders, the master builders, the apostles are God's chosen instruments for this task. We see this quite plainly in the New Testament writings. Paul dealt with false doctrines that were being taught, with divisions among the brethren, with sexual immorality and the like, and with local church leaders such as Diotrephes in the Third Epistle of John. This function has disappeared within the Body of Christ today leaving the Church in a vulnerable position.

Recognizing the Apostle

This, you might say, is all fine and dandy. But how do you tell who the real apostles are? Some may come shouting, "The foundation of the Church is laid on Jesus Christ." Is this person an apostle? I leave you with these thoughts concerning this matter, which will basically summarize this section on apostles.

You will recognize an apostle as one set apart, different and anointed. The apostle will speak God's Word with power and authority, with miracles, signs and wonders following, all according to the grace of God. The apostle's words will speak of Jesus Christ, the work on the cross and of the Lord's return. He will continually be preaching the gospel and have a love for the lost. The apostle's doctrine will be sound, always lined up with the Word. He will desire to see the Church built up and the saints perfected. He will have a larger vision for the Body of Christ, which extends to the city limits and beyond. The apostle seeks to unite local bodies for a common cause of reaching the lost.

Don't be too critical. For I believe that even as we speak God is raising up apostles whom He is supernaturally training. They will not be perfect. But if you are listening to what the Spirit of the Lord is saying, you will recognize them.

We will end our study of apostles here. There are other topics we could discuss, such as the baptism of the Holy Spirit, the working of miracles and signs and wonders and a host of others. I believe we will learn so much more of this office of apostle as God raises up the apostle in local churches and we experience the ministry of this office. The Church needs to go forward.

6

The Prophet

In recent years there has been much written and said about prophets. In some church circles and denominations, they do not believe in prophecy. In some charismatic circles, everyone wants to prophesy; everyone wants to be seen as a prophet. People write down predictions and prophesies they claim are from the Lord which never come to pass. Others prophesy with such a broad scope that it is almost meaningless, and sooner or later their "prophecies" are almost sure to happen. We have so few written and documented prophecies which have come to pass that most Christians wonder, "Are there true prophets of God today?"

This writer does not claim to be an authority on prophets or prophecy. It is not knowledge about prophets that is important here. What is important, I believe, is that God is trying to communicate to His Church that, yes, prophets are for today and they are vital for the proper functioning of the Body of Christ, that it is paramount that we find out who are God's prophets in our local bodies and that with God-given authority the office of prophet must be implemented.

In how many local churches throughout America is someone known as a prophet? I mean a true prophet, not someone who prophesies a lot. Most Christians right now could not make that distinction.

The biggest hindrance to the surfacing of the prophet in the Body of Christ comes from our own church leaders. When we studied the apostle, we learned that "God hath set some in the church, first apostles, secondarily prophets, thirdly teachers..." (1 Cor. 12:28). We also learned the foundation of the Church was laid by apostles and prophets by revelation through Jesus Christ. It is the religious leaders of today who would have to give up their high positions, their pulpits and their fame for someone whom God has chosen to place before them.

Following is a passage of Scripture that earmarks the greatest spiritual breakthrough for the advancement of Kingdom of God, the coming of Jesus Christ. It is about the prophet, John the Baptist.

The Prophet

And he came into all the country about Jordan, preaching the baptism of repentance for the remission of sins; as it is written in the book of the words of Esaias the prophet, saying, The voice of one crying in the wilderness, Prepare ye the way of the Lord, make His paths straight. Every valley shall be filled, and every mountain and hill shall be brought low; and the crooked shall be made straight, and the rough ways shall be made smooth; and all flesh shall see the salvation of God. Then said he to the multitude that came forth to be baptized of him, O generation of vipers, who hath warned you to flee from the wrath to come? Bring forth therefore fruits worthy of repentance, and begin not to say within yourselves, We have Abraham to our father: for I say unto you, That God is able of these stones to raise up children unto Abraham. And now also the axe is laid unto the root of the trees: every tree therefore which bringeth not forth good fruit is hewn down, and cast into the fire. And the people asked him, saying, What shall we do then? He answereth and saith unto them, He that hath two coats, let him impart to him that hath none; and he that hath meat, let him do likewise. Then came also publicans to be baptized, and said unto him, Master, what shall we do? And he said unto them, Exact no more than that which is appointed you. And the soldiers likewise demanded

A Church of Power Is Emerging

of him, saying, And what shall we do? And he said unto them, Do violence to no man, neither accuse any falsely; and be content with your wages. And as the people were in expectation, and all men mused in their hearts of John, whether he were the Christ, or not; John answered, saying unto them all, I indeed baptize you with water; but One mightier than I cometh, the latchet of whose shoes I am not worthy to unloose: He shall baptize you with the Holy Ghost and with fire: Whose fan is in His hand, and He will thoroughly purge His floor, and will gather the wheat into His garner; but the chaff He will burn with fire unquenchable. And many other things in his exhortation preached he unto the people. Luke 3:3-18

This passage reveals a great deal of the ministry of the prophet. As seen from the first two verses, the prophet will be a preacher, and it will be the Word of God that the prophet will uphold, just as John refers to the words of Isaiah. Be careful of so-called prophets who proclaim their own words, who have an arrogance toward the authority of the Word of God.

At the heart of the preaching comes forth the message of repentance. Most of the prophetic writings in the Scriptures deal with this one word, *repentance*. Jesus preached repentance. It simply is an exhortation to turn back to God, to get right with

The Prophet

God. This applies so aptly today. The Church needs to repent and get right with God, and so does the world.

The gifting of the prophet is a seer. Do not confuse this word with the occult seer, who is led by the spirit of the devil. The prophet sees supernaturally. He sees wickedness and corruption as God allows and directs him to see it. He then speaks forth God's word, under the inspiration of the Holy Spirit, concerning this sin. We see an example of this in verses 11 through 14, in which John told the people what they needed to do. We need prophets today who can expose, in explicit ways, the sin and corruption in the Body of Christ, especially among the leaders who are stiffling the Holy Spirit. This was a harsh word that John spoke, "O generation of vipers...."

Some church leaders refer to First Corinthians 14:3, "But he that prophesieth speaketh unto men to edification, and exhortation, and comfort." One prophesies to edify, to exhort and to comfort. This would normally be the purpose for prophesying among all Christians whom the Holy spirit inspires to prophesy. But not so with the man who holds the office of prophet, who has the mantle of prophet. Not only will the prophet strengthen and encourage and comfort the Body of Christ, but he will also reprove and rebuke and correct, as we saw with the call of Jeremiah "to root out, and to pull down, and to destroy, and to throw down, to build, and to plant" (Jer. 1:10).

We may not like what the prophet has to say. Pastors may cringe at the thought of giving liberty to the prophets to speak during the church service. The congregation may just stand up and walk out following the prophet's message. But this is what faith is all about, trusting in God and His Word and His messengers, trusting that in the long run the Kingdom of Heaven will be advanced, trusting that in Heaven you will be approved by God.

Prepare Ye the Way of the Lord

It is not that the prophet enjoys preaching repentance, bringing forth a word of reproof, but it is to prepare the way for the Lord. This is the main purpose of the prophet. It is the prophet who has been called by God to see that things are prepared for what the Lord is doing next. What is the Lord's way? How does the Lord want the Church to be built before He comes back for His Bride?

Church leaders too often have their own way plotted out, which leaves them with a heart too hard to hear the prophet speak. Remember, the prophet is a man after the Word of God, and he will be sure that what he speaks lines up with God's infallible Word. Repentance then becomes the key word to get us back on the *way*, back on track.

I have been involved over the past several years with prayer meetings in which laymen and pastors have come together from all different denominations and nondenominational churches to pray for revival. Repentance was often the theme as the Holy Spirit directed. However, I perceived that many who would repent for the whole Church always prayed the kind of prayer that blames others, that points to other churches as the source of sin, rather than believe that their own church had missed the mark. It would be the other pastors, the other members and the other denominations who were at fault. It reminds me of the Pharisee who stood up and prayed, "God, I thank Thee, that I am not as other men are, extortioners, unjust, adulterers, or even as this publican. I fast twice in the week, I give tithes of all that I possess" (Lk. 18:11-12). The prophet in the local church will see as God sees, will see the sin in the local church and will not be afraid to expose it.

The Lord is coming back for a glorious Church, a Church with *no* spots or wrinkles. The prophet will be used by God to help accomplish this work.

Notice in the passage from the Gospel of Luke that John the Baptist indicated when the Lord comes He will baptize with the Holy Ghost and with fire. That's what we are looking for, the fire to come down from Heaven, the same fire that fell when Elijah confronted the false prophets and all the people of Israel on Mount Carmel. Just as He did in the case of Elijah, God will use His prophets to prepare the way. The Church, however, has taken the stand that the Lord is with us, in our midst, and is prepared for a great move of God. In the book of Revelation, Jesus sent a letter to seven churches, and in closing He said, "Behold, I stand at the door, and knock: if any man hear My voice, and open the door, I will come in to him, and will sup with him, and he with Me" (Rev. 3:20). Here Jesus is portrayed as standing outside the Church. How sad. Is the Lord standing outside the door of your church? The Church needs prophets in this day and age who will continue to preach repentance and prepare the way for the Lord, because without the Lord being with us, we can do nothing.

The Testimony of Jesus

Now we come to the most important aspect of the prophet and of any true man of God. It is the testimony of Jesus. Notice in verses 15 and 16 of Luke 3 that all the people were wondering whether John the Baptist were the Christ. John, however, immediately took their eyes off himself and deferred to the One who was to follow him. In John 1:29, John the

Baptist said this about Jesus, "Behold the Lamb of God, which taketh away the sin of the world."

The main distinction between a true and false prophet is the testimony of Jesus as both Lord and Christ, the Savior of the world. The spirit of the devil will not testify to this fact. This is why this is such an important part of the calling of a prophet. Other Scriptures will bear this out.

And I fell at his feet to worship him. And he said unto me, See thou do it not: I am thy fellowservant, and of thy brethren that have the testimony of Jesus: worship God: for the testimony of Jesus is the spirit of prophecy. Revelation 19:10

To Him give all the prophets witness, that through His name whosoever believeth in Him shall receive remission of sins. Acts 10:43

The very nature of prophecy, of the spirit of the prophet, is to give testimony to Jesus and glorify His name. In our example, John did this without hesitation. Here lies our first and foremost test of a prophet, does he give testimony to himself, to man, to a great leader or to Jesus? How much does he speak of himself and his words and his ways? How much does he speak of Jesus, of His words, of His ways?

I'll always remember a man who was brought in to speak at a local church where I was a member in my early Christian days. Many thought this man was a prophet because he had a testimony of dying and going to Heaven, where he had received some divine power from God. He was then brought back to life after some 20 minutes. He had many good things to say. But never once did he speak of or testify to Jesus Christ. He spoke mostly of his dream and the divine power and capabilities that he had. I sensed something wrong and wondered, "was this man a true prophet of God, or was he a false prophet?"

The more that the Body of Christ has a foundation laid upon Jesus Christ, whereby Christians eat, breathe and sleep the life, the ways, and the words of Jesus, the less we will be led astray.

The Prophet's Role in the Church

The prophet is sometimes seen as a "Lone Ranger," someone who operates on his own. This is not to be the case for the New Testament prophet. As seen from our Scripture in Ephesians 4 on the fivefold ministry, men are gifted differently as the Lord wills, as apostles, prophets, evangelists and so forth, to perfect the saints so the Body of Christ can be built up. The prophet works together with these other called-out men to edify the Church. Now this is the way it should work. We have a slight problem today in that the Church does not want to accept the ministry of all five gifts. I believe there are evangelists, prophets and apostles who have been called by God and are right now being trained by the Lord. They are ready to serve in the Body of Christ as the Lord moves to raise up local bodies that embrace the fivefold ministry.

Two of the primary functions of a prophet in relationship to the Church are to lay the foundation of the Church in conjunction with the apostle, recognizing that the apostle is first, the prophet second, and to help perfect the saints for the work of ministry to edify the Body of Christ. You might ask, "How exactly does the prophet do this?" The prophet does this according to his gifting, much as we have already discussed. Following is a brief summary:

The prophet will be a preacher of what pertains to here and now. The prophet will uphold the Word of God, will have tremendous respect for the authority of the word of God. The prophet will not only preach and prophesy words of encouragement, exhortation and comfort, but also repentance to prepare the Body of Christ for the work of ministry and for the Lord's return. The prophet will also testify to Jesus Christ. He will always be pointing the people to the Lord and demanding the church give glory to Jesus Christ.

Following are some points we have not yet discussed:

A prophet will be a disciple. Just as apostles were disciples first, so too will prophets be disciples.

A prophet will be a man of God. The prophet will set an example for the Church by being a man of high moral and ethical standards. Prophets will set an example of prayer, of standing in the counsel of the Lord. They will not only declare the ways of God, but will uphold them. Brothers and sisters in the Lord, there are countless small but corrupt ways which are tolerated in the Body of Christ. The prophet will not stand for any sin, no matter how small. Every detail of the Word of God is important to the prophet.

A function of the New Testament prophet that I believe the Church has overlooked is using the prophetic gifting to lead others to Christ. An indication of this is seen in the following Scripture:

But if all prophesy, and there come in one that believeth not, or one unlearned, he is convinced of all, he is judged of all: and thus are the secrets of his heart made manifest; and so falling down on his face he will worship God, and report that God is in you of a truth. 1 Corinthians 14:24-25

Here prophecy is of benefit to open the heart of the unbeliever so that he will turn and call out to the

The Prophet

Lord. Another more detailed example of the use of the prophetic gifting is seen in the life of Jesus as He met the Samaritan woman at the well in the fourth chapter of the Gospel of John.

> *The woman saith unto Him, Sir, give me this water, that I thirst not, neither come hither to draw. Jesus saith unto her, Go, call thy husband, and come hither. The woman answered and said, I have no husband. Jesus said unto her, Thou hast well said, I have no husband: for thou hast had five husbands; and he whom thou now hast is not thy husband: in that saidst thou truly. The woman saith unto Him, Sir, I perceive that Thou art a prophet.... The woman then left her waterpot, and went her way into the city, and saith to the men, Come, see a Man, which told me all things that ever I did: is not this the Christ? Then they went out of the city, and came unto Him.* John 4:15-19; 28-30

Here the Lord used the prophetic ministry to cause this woman to believe on him. For all those who believe themselves to be prophets or those who desire to prophesy, there is no excuse for a lack of witnessing, or going out and proclaiming the gospel. Again, testifying of Jesus is the spirit of prophecy. I believe the New Testament prophet can and should use his spiritual gifting to lead many to

Jesus Christ and unto salvation. Exercise that gift you believe the Lord has given you.

Of course the prophet will also be used as a messenger. As Isaiah the prophet said, "Here am I; send me" (Is. 6:8). And so, prophets will be sent out. As the Old Testament prophets spoke unto the whole nation of Israel, there also will be some prophets today who will be anointed to speak unto the nations the message of God. They also will predict the future, as the prophet Agabus did when he prophesied to the Church of a severe famine to come (Acts 11:28).

What, if any, of the roles or characteristics of the Old Testament prophet have ended in New Testament times? Yes, there are some. First and foremost is the prophet's place of priority. The Lord has chosen the apostle to come first, the prophet second. Any New Testament prophet will be the first to uphold the Lord's decree.

Secondly, the prophet functions in relationship to the Church; this was not the case in the Old Testament. We have discussed this relationship above.

Thirdly, yet very significantly, is the role the Holy Spirit plays in prophecy in New Testament times. The fact that the Holy Spirit dwells within every believer affords every believer the opportunity to prophesy. All Christians are to eagerly desire to prophesy, as we see in First Corinthians 14. But all will prophesy according to the grace apportioned, and a greater portion is given to the prophets who hold the office of prophet and have the mantle of authority.

Because of the indwelling of the Holy Spirit in all believers, there is no longer the need to go to someone else for divine direction. We all can seek the Lord and His will for our lives. If you have a call on your life, then the Lord will speak to you directly. Don't be persuaded by those who pretend to prophesy and "prophesy" great things over all. Remember, only *some* will be apostles; only *some* will be prophets. However, there is nothing wrong with wise counsel from other men of God. These men can help discern whether you have truly heard from God.

Let us look at an example in the Old Testament regarding this.

And when Moses' father-in-law saw all that he did to the people, he said, What is this thing that thou doest to the people? why sittest thou thyself alone, and all the people stand by thee from morning unto even? And Moses said unto his father-in-law, Because the people come unto me to inquire of God: when they have a matter, they come unto me; and I judge between one and another, and I do make them know the statutes of God, and His laws. Exodus 18:14-16

Here the people sought Moses for direction and guidance. It was Moses who spoke directly with God.

No Christian need approach his or her pastor, teacher, a prophet or anyone to inquire of God. We can do that directly through the Holy Spirit. It was Jesus who said He would send the *comforter*, or *counselor*. No church need look to their pastor or church leaders for direction, we have it already recorded in the Word of God.

I have heard some pastors say their church specializes in, say, healing or teaching when at the same time they neglect the "great commission." These church pastors believe they hear from God when in fact they haven't. They are deceiving you. The business of every local church is what the Bible declares and not what man says.

The prophet receives revelation concerning Jesus Christ and the Word of God. He receives a clearer understanding of the Word of God and of its mysteries to relate to the Body of Christ, to keep the church on course and focused on Christ, not to lead them off in some other direction.

This ends our study of the role of the New Testament prophet. I have covered those areas into which I believe the Lord has given me some insight. This is only a taste of the life of a prophet.

There is one more area of concern which I will briefly cover. It is finding out who the real prophets of God are and implementing their office in the local body.

Implementing the Office of the New Testament Prophet

For a church leader, the first step is to come to the place where you can say, "I am going to seek out God's anointed prophets and then allow them to operate in this local body with the authority God has given them."

These are some things that may be going through your mind: How will I find out who the true prophets are? Will others be jealous and cause strife within the body? If the prophet is allowed to speak and does expose the sins of the people and of the local church, there will be many upset members who might just leave. What about all of our bills, the church mortgage and the payroll? Will we be able to survive if many leave? Will I myself risk being thrown out? There are countless reasons why any church pastor or leader would just throw up his or her hands and say, "It just isn't worth it."

Brothers and sisters in the Lord, God's word is always worth it. His plan for His Church is a perfect plan. Our problem is that we are, "in the natural" so much that the way we think the Church should be run and operate is not the plan of the Lord. We compare too much and use our eyes too much, instead of being obedient and walking by faith.

Let's now consider finding out who the real prophets are in the local church, if any. Where do you begin? Begin by saying to your people, "All those who believe that God has called them out to be a prophet, please come forward." Of course you make the distinction between the office of a prophet and the many who will have faith to prophesy. Listen carefully to the testimony of each person. Remember, the Lord "hath set some in the church, first apostles, secondarily prophets..." (1 Cor. 12:28). The Lord hath set them in the Church—man does not place them at his convenience. In the more charismatic churches you may have half your congregation come forward at this time. That's okay.

Then, let them talk. Let them speak of the things that God may have revealed to them. Don't try to lead them by questioning them. Why? Because it is that the true prophet will teach us, not that we will teach them. What a true prophet says will be relevant and important. Also, if there is no

The Prophet

testimony of Jesus Christ, then we know the person is not a prophet. If there is no reference to Scripture, beware. A prophet upholds the Word of God. If what the person says does not line up with Scripture, then he or she has not heard from God. At this point you may perceive the grace of God that is upon someone, as the apostles in Jerusalem perceived the grace of God that was upon Paul and received him into their fellowship.

Now you might want to ask some pertinent questions like, "What do you believe is the function of a New Testament prophet?" You basically are asking this person to apply for a job, and he should full well know what his function will be, especially in relationship to the church. This we have discussed already.

The Word of God says you will know them by their fruit. This includes all fruit, I believe—the fruit of the Spirit, the fruit of their ministry and the fruit of their words. Please, we are not looking for credentials and degrees. Of what kinds of ministry has this person been a part? What prophecies or words from God has this person already spoken? Have the prophecies come to pass?

If the individual is personally known then he should be someone of high repute. The prophet should be a man of God. This would include being a true disciple, a man of moral integrity and a man of prayer. We need to proceed with caution here, because I believe there will be many rising prophets who have not matured because of a lack of training in some areas. Don't be too critical. There will be a period of trial and error since we have not had recognized prophets ministering at the local level in a long time.

Now we have come to the point of selection. Once you have chose, then implement their calling. Let the whole congregation know who they are and that now comes a time of trial. This is when the fear of God should be instilled into the hearts of the prophets. In Old Testament times, the prophet who spoke falsely in the name of God was stoned to death. Today, because of the indwelling of the Holy Spirit all Christians have the capacity to prophesy according to the grace of God, but the prophet to a greater extent, of course because of his calling. Mistakes will be made, but we no longer need to stone all those who speak out of the flesh. However, since what the prophet speaks should be taken seriously by the whole congregation and acted upon, the prophet should be warned not to speak carelessly in the name of the Lord, lest he lose his liberty to speak. Naturally the messages and words from the prophet need to be tested according to the Word of God and by discernment.

The Prophet

In no way do I claim to be an authority on this subject of prophets; I simply give some recommendations. I encourage you to go forward by faith.

7

The Evangelist

Quite frankly, I believe the average local church is not a soul-winning body of believers. Sad, but true. One of the greatest challenges for the Church today is to take a congregation and so equip it that souls are daily being brought into the Kingdom of God. Take a moment to reflect on what I just said. Doesn't this sound exciting? Is it not scriptural? Wouldn't you personally want to be a part of such a church? Most churches leave this work up to a pastor, a teacher or even the youth minister, when according to biblical order they need an evangelist.

Jesus Was an Evangelist

Yes! Jesus was an evangelist. Throughout our Lord's earthly ministry He was constantly soul winning. He came preaching, "The time has come. the Kingdom of God is near. Repent and believe the good news!" From village to village Jesus went seeking out the lost. We get a glimpse of the heart of Jesus in Luke 4:42-44 (NIV):

At daybreak Jesus went out to a solitary place. The people were looking for Him and when they came to where He was, they tried to keep Him from leaving them. But He said, "I must preach the good news of the Kingdom of God to the other towns also, because that is why I was sent." And He kept on preaching in the synagogues of Judea.

It is rather easy to surmise that Jesus was in prayer when the towns people approached Him. What was the conversation that Jesus had with the Father? Did it concern the lost? We see that Jesus was compelled to go on. Lost souls no doubt were heavily upon the heart of our Lord. It was for this cause that He called others to follow Him, to become fishers of men. The Lord would equip others to continue His ministry.

For three years Jesus personally trained the Twelve and others. He taught them how to teach and preach on the Kingdom and to heal the sick and cast out demons. Then He sent them out, first the Twelve and then 70 others, to try out their ability to win souls. The Bible doesn't tell us how the disciples went out, whether they were happy or excited or whether they dragged their feet while Jesus admonished them to go forth. However, we do know that the disciples returned with joy (Lk. 10:17). It was a joy to share the message of salvation. It was a joy to pray with the sick and bring deliverance to those possessed by demons. It was a joy to serve the Lord. This task of preaching the gospel was so important that Jesus left the apostles with specific instructions before He ascended, to "go and make disciples of all nations," to go into all the world and preach the good news to all creation. This was a command. This was the "Great Commission."

The Great Omission

Where does your local church fit into this Great Commission? Or doesn't it? Proverbs 11:30 says, "The fruit of the righteous is a tree of life; and he that winneth souls is wise." A wise man will win souls into the Kingdom. A spiritually wise church will be a soul-winning church. There seems to be an implication in this passage that the fruit that comes from winning souls is a tree of life. Is the fruit in the life of your local body a tree of life, ever growing and sprouting forth fruit?

Today's Church is well aware of the Great Commission. Yet what we have is a *great omission*. The reason for this great omission is that we have deleted the "C" from *commission*; we have deleted Christ as the head of the Church. Christ has been removed as the head of many churches, because we have failed to build the Church according to the plans of the Lord, using the fivefold ministry. Where is the evangelist to spearhead our evangelistic ministries and keep the body focused on the Great Commission? Where is the evangelist to constantly exhort the people to go out to win souls?

The Work of an Evangelist

Yes, the evangelist is a "species" close to extinction. In some church circles the word *evangelism* is frightening and has been replaced with words like *renewal* or *outreach*. These words seem more palatable for the people and conform more to their level of sharing the gospel. These people, these churches, these denominations have separated themselves from the Word of God to suit their own ways, beliefs and life styles. They have their own concept of evangelism rather than a biblical one.

I suggest you find an evangelist. He will tell you what a biblical way of sharing our faith is. He will tell you to read the first eight chapters of the Book of Acts to get a clear picture of how the early Church was growing by leaps and bounds. This is what you will find: The early Church was a church of prayer. It was a Church obedient in witnessing and proclaiming the gospel, boldly going forth with the good news even in the midst of persecution. It was a Church that went into the public markets and from house to house, never ceasing to preach the gospel. It was a Church endued with power, through which people were being saved daily.

Yes, I do not mind saying this again: Find for yourself an evangelist. His job is to preach the gospel. His job is to perfect the saints for the work of the ministry as indicated in Ephesians 4:11-12; this would be to equip the saints to do the work of an evangelist, to train the entire body to preach and be effective witnesses of the gospel, to take them out into the streets to exercise their faith and carry out the Great Commission. His job is to constantly keep the church thinking about lost souls and places where they may find them. All this and more is the job of the evangelist, so that the church would be built up. Because the evangelist is missing in the life of most churches, we are left a Church today without a Great Commission.

Here is an example I would like you to ponder. Suppose two people started a church, and every year all those in the church were to lead two others to the Lord. After one year you would have six members. Each of these would now lead two more people to the Lord the next year. How many members would this congregation have after ten years? The answer is staggering—over 100,000. If we could but teach every member to share the gospel, no telling how many of our cities could be won into the Kingdom of God. This is where the evangelist fits in.

Now, let me share with you for a moment what I believe is the greatest hindrance to the going forth of the gospel. It is *fear*. It is fear of sharing the gospel, fear of not knowing how to share the gospel, fear of praying with someone, fear of witnessing to a stranger, fear of speaking the name of Jesus in public, fear of being labeled a Christian fanatic by peers, fear of rejection, fear of going into the inner city and being physically harmed, fear of losing one's life and all of one's precious possessions for the sake of the gospel. Fear is what the devil puts into your mind to thwart the Lord's plan of furthering the Kingdom of God in your city. The Bible says, however,

> *For God hath not given us the spirit of fear; but of power, and of love, and of a sound mind. Be not thou therefore ashamed of the testimony of our Lord, nor of me his prisoner: but be thou partaker of the afflictions of the gospel according to the power of God.... 2 Timothy 1:7-8.*

Here Paul addresses Timothy to stir him up and exhort him. This passage applies to all Christians. In this Scripture we see the Holy Spirit working within all believers as they relate to the gospel, giving them *power* to preach the gospel and to testify to the Lord, *love* so that we can love the lost as Jesus loves them and a *sound* mind, referring to what the Holy Spirit desires, not what our minds want to do, even to the point of suffering.

Folks, are you led around by the devil like a dog on a leash, because of fear? Or are you led by the Holy Spirit? The next section on the witness will help you.

The Witness

This will most likely be a new concept for you, but I share this with you so that your fear of witnessing might be overcome. Webster's Dictionary defines a *witness* as "a person who has observed a certain event; a person who testifies to this observation." The event of importance to a Christian, of course, is the death of Jesus Christ and His resurrection from the grave. Jesus is alive as He claimed. This is confirmed by the following Scripture:

Then Peter and the other apostles answered and said, We ought to obey God rather than men. The God of our fathers raised up Jesus, whom ye slew and hanged on a tree. Him hath God exalted with His right hand to be a Prince and a Savior, for to give repentance to Israel, and forgiveness of sins. And we are His witnesses of these things;

A Church of Power Is Emerging

and so is also the Holy Ghost, whom God hath given to them that obey Him. Acts 5:29-32

The actual number of witnesses to this event were relatively few, namely, the apostles and some other disciples and, of course, the Holy Spirit. How many eye witnesses are there alive today? The answer is not one earthly man. However, there is still one witness on the face of the earth, the Holy Spirit. But the Holy Spirit does not speak audibly to unbelievers; He needs a spokesman.

"He that believeth on the Son of God hath the witness in Himself..." (1 John 5:10). Every Christian who has by faith been reconciled to God through Jesus Christ has now become a witness, has the witness in him, namely, the Holy Spirit. What is the main purpose for which He, the Holy Spirit, was sent? "But when the Comforter is come, whom I will send unto you from the Father, even the Spirit of truth, which proceedeth from the Father, He shall testify of Me..." (Jn. 15:26). The Comforter, the Holy Spirit, was sent to testify, to witness concerning Jesus Christ and, most specifically, to the work of the cross and of the resurrection from the dead.

So! What does all of this mean? By faith in Jesus Christ we were born again. At that time we received the Holy Spirit, who now dwells within us. We were not a witness to the actual death of Christ, but He that now lives within us was. His purpose is to testify to the death and resurrection of our Lord, and it now should become our purpose. We need to understand that when we go out to preach the gospel and share our faith in the living Christ, we do not go out alone, under intimidation and in fear and weakness. No! We go out under the *power* of the Holy Spirit. We no longer need to have fear about what to say or preach or about casting out demons. Why? Because we have the Holy Spirit with us to lead us and guide us. He has witnessed all that Jesus has taught and preached, all the works and all the miracles that Jesus had ever done. The Holy Spirit does not lack for anything. It is He who comforts us. The next time you go out to preach or witness trust in Him who dwells within you. Every Christian has this same potential within them.

The Militant Church

One night I had taken a close brother in the Lord home to his apartment. We sat in the car just talking about the Lord. We were parked on one side of a park, and looking down another side, I could see a church with which I was familiar. A question arose in my mind. I turned to my friend and asked him, "Who do you think is in possession of this territory, meaning the park and all the houses that surround it—the Lord or the devil?" My brother did not know.

A Church of Power Is Emerging

I suggested we determine this by simply stating that if on one street 51 percent or more of the families were saved, that street belonged to the Lord. If not, then that street belonged to the devil. If three of the four streets that bordered the park belonged to the Lord, then the park belonged to the Kingdom of God; otherwise it was the devil's territory. I pondered this for a time and wondered how many streets throughout the city were controlled by the devil. My conclusion was that almost every street and park in that city were controlled by the devil. Furthermore, to face reality, the whole city was the devil's territory. The devil was in control, and he and his demons possessed the land. Just about every place that I could think of, including the church, was completely engulfed by the enemy. This thought, I must say, rather irritated me.

What then came to my mind was that the church needed to get militant. The following Scripture popped into my mind: "And from the days of John the Baptist until now the Kingdom of heaven suffereth violence, and the violent take it by force" (Mt. 11:12).

This earth was the creation of the Lord. But because the devil has blinded the minds of unbelievers, much of the earth is the possession of the devil and all of his demonic followers. The devil has set up his own kingdoms in the world. Our cities are under the control of the devil. Large institutions are controlled by the devil. Business offices are under the influence of the devil. Our schools and universities are controlled by the devil. Medical clinics are controlled by the devil. On and on it goes, including nearly every house, street corner and park.

Brothers and sisters in the Lord, it is time for the army of the Lord to arise, it is time for the Church to get violent, it is time we take back our cities. It is time the Church takes evangelism seriously, it is time we sing, "Onward Christian soldiers, marching as to war, with the cross of Jesus going on before. Christ, the royal Master, leads against the foe, forward into battle see His banners go,"[1] and sing it with meaning. We need to lay out a plan to go house to house, street to street, neighborhood to neighborhood with the gospel message, until we win back our cities. The Church must become militant, it desperately needs the gift the Lord has given to it—the evangelist.

---

1. ©1864, Sabine Baring-Gould.

8

The Pastor

I believe there are many pastors who are truly dedicated to the Lord and His work. These pastors do everything they can to be servants and to feed their flock. They love the sheep.

Pastor, if you believe the Church is without power and has missed the mark, what are you going to do? If you believe your church has shunned its responsibility of preaching the gospel and healing the sick and casting out demons, then what is your next step? If you are convinced that you have not made true disciples of your flock, how are you going to proceed? And if you now believe in the fivefold ministry and that, in fact, apostles and prophets are important today in laying the foundation of the

Church, will you then submit yourself to God's plan for building the Church?

This book was not meant to be an exhaustive study of each part of the fivefold ministry. I have not covered the ministry of the teacher, but I would like to cover just a few topics concerning the pastor.

There is much confusion in the Church today as to who should feed and oversee the flock—pastors, elders or bishops. Elders are often thought of as deacons and used in that same capacity in many denominations. Bishops are given a higher authority in some denominations, yet in others, they are considered to be just an elder. This is a very important point, because we need to know whom God has appointed as the leaders of the Church, who is to shepherd the flock, thus making those Scriptures meaningful which refer to these men. Now, what exactly is the case? Who is the shepherd of the flock?

Let's read Acts 14:20b-23.

...and the next day he [Paul] departed with Barnabas to Derbe. And when they had preached the gospel to that city, and had taught many, they returned again to Lystra, and to Iconium, and Antioch, confirming the souls of the disciples, and exhorting them to continue in the faith, and that we must through much tribulation enter

into the kingdom of God. And when they had ordained them elders in every church, and had prayed with fasting, they commended them to the Lord, on whom they believed.

It was the elders who were designated as the first leaders over the local churches in each of these cities. To further support this fact we read as Paul addresses Titus,

For this cause I left thee in Crete, that thou shouldest set in order the things that are wanting, and ordain elders in every city, as I had appointed thee: if any be blameless, the husband of one wife, having faithful children not accused of riot or unruly. For a bishop must be blameless, as the steward of God; not selfwilled, not soon angry, not given to wine, no striker, not given to filthy lucre; but a lover of hospitality, a lover of good men, sober, just, holy, temperate; holding fast the faithful word as he hath been taught, that he may be able by sound doctrine both to exhort and to convince the gainsayers. Titus 1:5-9

Again, it was elders who were ordained as the leaders over these local churches. Verse 7 refers to these elders as bishops. So we see elders are the same as bishops. The qualifications that are listed here are almost the same as those listed in First Timothy 3:1-7, which is the passage to which we often refer for the qualifications of a pastor. Actually the passage refers to the qualifications of a bishop, "...If a man desire the office of a bishop, he desireth a good work. A bishop then must be..." (1 Tim. 3:1-2). So what we may have commonly thought to be a passage referring to *pastor*, refers to *bishop* or *elder*. The apostle Peter makes this remark:

> *The elders which are among you I exhort, who am also an elder, and a witness of the sufferings of Christ, and also a partaker of the glory that shall be revealed: feed the flock of God which is among you, taking the oversight thereof, not by constraint, but willingly; not for filthy lucre, but of a ready mind....* 1 Peter 5:1-2

This Scripture completes the picture for us: Elders were to feed the flock of sheep and were to act as shepherds over the flock God had entrusted to them. We now see that in the early Church *elders* was the name most commonly used of leaders and shepherds of the flock and that another name for elder was *bishop*. Notice the plurality of elders spoken of in these Scriptures. Throughout the New Testament, there were always more than one elder appointed to shepherd and oversee the flock. This was the Lord's plan. We will see the importance of this in the next chapter on church government. Where did *pastor* come from? I really don't know. We have only one Scripture in the Word of God using *pastor*,

The Pastor

Ephesians 4:11, "And He gave...some, pastors...." the Interlinear Greek-English Version uses the word *shepherd* for pastor: "...and some shepherds and teachers." Various terms could have come into existence to indicate the person, the title, the function or job.

The important thing is to understand that elder, bishop, pastor and overseer all relate to the same position, that of shepherd of the flock. So when we read the New Testament we will not be confused by what our own church terminology is, and we will be able to appropriately interpret Scripture to recognize how the Lord is building the Church.

There are three brief points I would like to bring out regarding the shepherd. Regarding the first two, I would like us to read from the Gospel of John, chapter 10. This of course is one of the great passages on shepherding, portraying Jesus as the Good Shepherd.

> *I am the Good Shepherd: the Good Shepherd giveth His life for the sheep. But he that is an hireling, and not the shepherd, whose own the sheep are not, seeth the wolf coming, and leaveth the sheep, and fleeth: and the wolf catcheth them, and scattereth the sheep. The hireling fleeth, because he is an hireling, and careth not for the sheep. I am the Good Shepherd, and know My sheep, and am known of Mine.* John 10:11-14

Jesus knew His sheep. Every one of the sheep was equally important to Jesus. There was no favoritism. Not only did Jesus personally know each sheep, but each sheep knew Him. They knew His voice so that when He spoke, they paid attention. Likewise, any shepherd should personally know those members in his fold, and they should know him. It is vital that individuals and families in the Body of Christ be ministered to, that no one is left out of being cared for and ministered to. If someone in the church were without food, then an elder should be aware of it; if someone were sick, the elders should come and pray; if anyone were in need, an elder should be there.

This was one reason for multiple eldership in the local church, to respond and care for all the needs in the congregation and to know all the sheep by name. As churches grew in size, there would be a need for more elders. Too often in some of our churches with large membership the sheep are ignored, uncared for and left out. The poor, the sick, the needy, those with problems are unattended to. Jesus said to Peter, "Feed My sheep." It is a shame today that many of the Lord's sheep are starving because the shepherds are not feeding them.

The second point we would make from this Scripture is that Jesus cared for His sheep. Jesus

The Pastor

came willingly, not for pay. He desired to be a servant, not to be served. Jesus was willing to lay down His life for the sheep. Unfortunately, what we have today in some churches are hirelings, hired servants. In many denominations when help is needed, the senior pastor or some board or higher authority will look at resumes to find a so-called qualified person to fill the position. For a set salary this person then is hired. He usually is from outside the area and will know none of the sheep. (It is interesting to look at the definition of *hireling* in Webster's Dictionary. A hireling is someone with merely mercenary interest in the job for which he has been paid. *Mercenary* means "desiring gain.") Some of these hired pastors (using today's terminology) take a position because they are without a job or maybe there are better fringe benefits or a higher salary; sometimes it is a move up the religious ladder. But do they care for the sheep? In the New Testament the elders were chosen from among the local body. They would already know the sheep. The apostles would be able to discern whether they truly cared for the sheep before appointing them. The scriptural way is always better than man's way.

For our third point I would like us to return to First Peter 5:2-3. Peter, referring to the elders, says this:

Feed the flock of God which is among you, taking the oversight thereof, not by constraint, but willingly; not for filthy lucre, but of a ready mind; neither as being lords over God's heritage, but being ensamples to the flock.

Peter exhorts the elders to be examples to the flock. Jesus did not lord it over His disciples, giving them commands to go out and do things and whipping them into shape. No, He Himself went out and did the works of God, and His disciples watched and followed. If elders were to lead the people, how better to lead them than by setting an example for them. Jesus is the prime example for any shepherd. By studying the life of Christ we can make some very clear and accurate statements about the ministry of an elder.

An elder should blend prayer and ministry of the Word. To minister without prayer is to lean on self and not the Lord. When the leaders pray, the people will pray. When the elders are hungry for revival, the people will be too. As an elder, you don't have to be the best and pray the most, you only need to set an example, to lead.

Elders are first of all disciples, and as such they should be out preaching the gospel, healing the sick and training others in the works of Christ. Pastors should not be fearful, but bold in proclaiming the good news. The elders do not have to be an evangelist in the church, but they should set a good example for the sheep. Pastor, staying inside and administering and counseling and teaching is not setting the right example for your people. Jesus was the right example.

9

Church Government

The God we serve is not a God of chaos, but a God of order. The local church body was meant to be governed, to be ruled, to have leadership from its inception. Jesus Christ was to be the Head, He was to rule over the Church as part of the Kingdom of God. Jesus would lead and direct and build the Church. The Church was not to become the vision or imagination of man, but it was to be molded into a beautiful bride according to the pattern of the Lord.

Now listen very carefully. You may think that Jesus is the Head of your church, you may think that

A Church of Power Is Emerging

Jesus is in charge, but you are sadly mistaken. The church may appear to you to be a beautiful church, a scripturally based church, a church with great Sunday worship, a church in which the pastor and the people love the Lord, a church that is growing, *but* beneath all of this lies a "system of error." What do I mean? I mean that for hundreds of years local churches have been governed under a system of error by which man has set himself up to rule over the people. This is a monarchy, in which man rules, instead of a theocracy, in which God rules.

Let me explain. In some cases there is an outright monarchy, in which one man has set himself up to rule over the people. In other situations there are presbyters or the congregation appoints the pastor(s). However, even in many of these situations, because of the pastor's credentials and biblical knowledge, he still dominates spiritually and controls the body that has appointed him or her. Spiritually, these churches take on a monarchy rule.

Let us return to Ephesians 4:11-14.

And He gave some, apostles; and some, prophets; and some evangelists; and some, pastors and teachers; for the perfecting of the saints, for the work of the ministry, for the edifying of the body of Christ: till we all come in the unity of the faith, and the knowledge of the Son of God, unto a perfect man, unto the measure of the stature of the fulness of Christ: that we henceforth be no more children, tossed to and fro, and carried about with every wind of doctrine, by the sleight of men, and cunning craftiness, whereby they lie in wait to deceive....

The last verse in the Interlinear Greek-English New Testament reads,

...that no longer we may be infants, being tossed and carried about by every wind of the teaching in the sleight of men, in craftiness with a view to the systematizing of error....

The phrasing of the last few words is so graphic, "with a view to the systematizing of error." The fivefold ministry was not only to perfect the saints, but to keep the saints from crafty men who in their cunningness would set up a "system of error" within the Church. These crafty men have a "view" toward error; their hearts and minds are set on their own ways and not the ways of the Lord. With a lack of the fivefold ministry, especially apostles and prophets who lay the foundation, a system of error in the church government soon emerges. As we mentioned before, in many local churches the pattern is that one man, the pastor, spiritually controls the church. This is what is prevalent today throughout the Church.

We now will look at existing church government, and I will share with you the problems that have arisen because of a system of error in church government. Then we will examine in the Word of God how the church government should be set up and how it should operate. We will see the advantages of governing a church in a scriptural theocratic fashion.

Church Government Today

A common order of church government in the United States is one in which a pastor shepherds and rules over the flock. There may be an associate pastor or pastors who assist him, but they have a lesser capacity and are under the control of the senior pastor. In some churches the pastor will have appointed elders to have a function similar to that of associates. The head or senior pastor may be self-appointed, meaning he established the church, or he may have been set in place by a larger organization which oversees the pastor in some respects. In most cases this still leaves the pastor with supreme spiritual authority over the local body.

There are churches ruled by one man, the pastor, which take the example of Moses ruling over the Israelites as the scriptural basis for this type of government. Moses, after being approached by his father-in-law, Jethro, appointed others under him to be over thousands, hundreds and so forth; these were to hear the problems and meet the needs of the people. Today these people are termed assistant pastors or elders in the church. But it was Moses who heard directly from God and spoke to the people, so this type of pastor today likewise sees himself as the one who is to hear from God and direct and lead the people. Some pastors see themselves as "God's anointed," God's appointed leader to whom everyone should submit.

Is this the way the local church should be governed?

First, let's consider that the church is not of the Old Testament but the New Testament. The way in which God governed His people in the Old Testament—under prophets and priests and kings—is not the same as in the New Testament. The example of Moses is a good example to follow in the delegation of duties, as the appointment of deacons in the New Testament. But this was not God's plan for government in the New Testament. The Lord had a new plan: power and authority over the Kingdom of God would be exercised through the church, not the nation of Israel. He Himself chose the apostles to be first. The apostles would be instrumental in laying the foundation of a church. It was the apostles who would appoint elders, multiple pastors, over each local body.

There is not one church in the entire New Testament which had the "traditional" one-pastor form of church government. There is not one person called pastor who was referred to as the head of the local church. There is no Scripture that says in the church God set first the pastor. When a pastor has been set up in a church as the head man, that local church is not a theocracy but a monarchy.

As we have already seen, it was the apostles who appointed elders (pastors) in every church. Thus, God set in place the church leadership through His servants the apostles. This is a theocracy. Pastors today are for the most part self-appointed or set in place by a higher authority, a presbytery or the congregation itself. Most of these churches do not believe in apostles, let alone submit to the apostles' authority.

I have heard some pastors say they are the apostle in their church since they founded it. Founding a church does not constitute being an apostle. Anyone can gather a group of believers and start his or her own church. But is the gospel preached? Have miracles, signs and wonders followed the preaching of the gospel? Is the congregation primarily made up of new believers? Has the foundation been laid scripturally with an emphasis on Christ? Are disciples being made? Are the works of Christ becoming manifest? Is the right government being set in place? Has the apostle left to begin a new work elsewhere? These are the markings of an apostolic work. But in such cases, the answer to these questions is almost assuredly *no*!

The apostles always appointed multiple elders or pastors over the flock. No church is reported in the New Testament as having only one pastor or elder. We saw some of the main reasons for this in the previous section. To be the sole pastor and leader in charge is to usurp authority, to seize and hold a position of authority which rightfully belongs to another, namely, our Lord Jesus Christ.

Let me briefly summarize. An erroneous system of government has been set up in the Church. There has evolved a church system in which one man usurps authority from the Lord and sets himself up as the "pastor" or "spiritual leader" in charge. Such is prevalent today as the "traditional church," a monarchical church, in which one man rules.

What problems have arisen out of this unscriptural monarchical type of church government?

1. The pastor does everything: He preaches, leads spiritually, oversees church programs, administers, handles business affairs, counsels and so forth.

   The result: the pastor becomes overtaxed with administrative duties and often neglects prayer and the ministry of the Word of God. As the congregation grows, the sheep are neglected more and more. Pastoral breakdowns sometimes occur.

2. The pastor performs all the spiritual functions in the body, especially during the church services. He preaches, prays, prophesies, heals the sick and so forth.

The result: The people look to the pastor, and may even idolize him, as being everything to all the people. Consequently, the spiritual gifts that the Lord has given to others never surface. The Body of Christ never comes to its full potential.

3. Applying the "Moses concept" of church government, the pastor is to hear from God and lead and direct the flock. He becomes "God's anointed." Everything he or she does is deemed to be right. Now, it is true the sheep need to be led; they need to be directed. The problem is the pastor may always believe he has heard from God. Based on a word in prayer or a vision, dream or prophecy, he may take the whole flock off on some tangent, believing it is God's will, when in fact it opposes the Word of God.

For example, the pastor may focus the church on a particular ministry. Some churches have specialized in healing or teaching. In some churches music becomes the highlight of church activity. Counseling is emphasized today. Many churches have started schools. No doubt you can add to this list. The pastor, in his pastoral and teaching orientation, will take the church down a similar path.

The result: the authority of the Word of God takes a second place to the pastor who "hears from God." Ministries and programs are developed, while the Great Commission is put on a shelf. The business of the church changes to suit man, instead of lining up with the Bible.

4. With the hiring of elders or assistant pastors to work under the senior pastor, we have what Jesus referred to as hirelings caring for the sheep. I understand this is stretching the application, but there may be an associate who has a different motive from one of caring for the sheep. For example, we have countless Bible college graduates who are desperately looking for a job and will take almost any pastoral position. Many are looking to get ahead in the religious world and see this position as a stepping stone.

As a hireling, the assistant pastor basically is controlled by the senior pastor. He must submit to the senior pastor and is in a delicate position to approach the pastor if he feels the senior pastor is doing something unscriptural, whether it be in the pastor's personal life or with the church's programs.

The result: The sheep are not properly attended to nor cared for. Also, the pastor is at greater liberty to lead the flock astray. This is why many denominations instituted deacon boards and the like, to govern the pastor.

5. Others called to the fivefold ministry will be suppressed because the pastor will try to maintain control.

The result: Without apostles and prophets, a church will have a faulty foundation. The church will not be finely focused on Jesus Christ and the works of Christ. Prayer and scriptural ministries often will be lacking, especially evangelistic ministries. The saints seldom will be properly trained so that they can mature and become real disciples of the Lord. There will be a system of error by which Christ never becomes the true Head of the church and the Holy Spirit is always being stiffled. The power of God will rarely become manifest.

Those new churches sprouting up where God has begun to move powerfully must take heed.

6. There will be no check and balance in the church. There is no one in the fivefold ministry to make the pastor accountable. The assistant pastors cannot check on the pastor because he has hired them and can fire them.

The result: Pride, jealousy, greed and other sins can easily set in. Pride would cause the pastor to believe the church revolves around him; jealousy would thwart the anointing that is upon someone else in the body; greed would motivate the pastor to promote church growth and acquire wealth so that he makes a name for himself. Lustful sins also surface when there is no one to confront the pastor.

There are many more problems that exist in the 20th-century Church, many of them attributed to a monarchical system of church rule. The Church will continue to have "a view to the systematizing of error" until God's government, a theocracy, is set in place. Let's take a look at God's plan for church government.

God's Plan of Government

God's form of government is a theocracy, whereby God rules. God can rule only when those who rule over the Church have been duly appointed and set in place by God. Consider the first Church, the church at Jerusalem. Who were the leaders? The following passage will tell us.

A Church of Power Is Emerging

And certain men which came down [to Antioch] *from Judaea taught the brethren, and said, Except ye be circumcised after the manner of Moses, ye cannot be saved. When therefore Paul and Barnabas had no small dissension and disputation with them, they determined that Paul and Barnabas, and certain other of them, should go up to Jerusalem unto the apostles and elders about this question.... And the apostles and elders* [at Jerusalem] *came together for to consider of this matter.* Acts 15:1-2,6

The matter was settled, the Gentiles did not need to be circumcised and the whole Church was pleased.

The circumcision of the Gentiles was no small matter at this time. At the heart of the dispute was God's plan of salvation. Was salvation for Jew only or for the Jew and the Gentile? What was the means of salvation—did salvation come through circumcision or through faith in Jesus Christ?

It was the apostles who met with the elders to resolve the issue. In the early Church these were the leaders who made the decisions. There was not *one* pastor (elder), but many at Jerusalem.

This is an example of a theocratic form of government. This was not a monarchy, whereby one man, the pastor, made the decision. Nor was it a democracy whereby the people made the decision. God had chosen and set aside His apostles, and He had appointed elders through His vessels the apostles. The elders and apostles made the decisions together in the early Church. As time progressed more prophets and evangelists rose up, and I believe they also contributed to church leadership. As the apostles and prophets traveled, the church government was left in the hands of the elders. Each local church became autonomous. The elders governed the church, but they always taught and equipped the saints in a relationship of co-submission with the apostles and prophets who had laid the foundation.

We have mentioned three main points concerning the appointment of elders in the local body; first, apostles appointed the elders; secondly, there were always multiple elders; and thirdly, all the elders had equal authority. What advantages does this type of government have over today's conventional church system of one presiding pastor?

When we consider the apostles who appoint the elders, we must remember that it was the apostle(s) who laid the foundation for a particular church. Many were saved through the preaching of the apostle(s). The maturity and perfecting of the saints also was due to the apostle's teaching. The apostles, or apostle and prophet, had become spiritual fathers to these people and dearly cared for them. Their motivation in the selecting of elders was pure and unselfish. They would be moving on, separating themselves from any personal gain in that local congregation. They desired the best for the church that they had established. Who would be better than the apostles to appoint the elders to carry on with God's work?

Paul wrote letters to the churches he helped establish. In the letters we see words of thanksgiving for them, words of encouragement, words to strengthen and words of exhortation. We also see correction and rebuke—but we never see Paul using his position to manipulate or control these churches. Following is a typical example of Paul's writing to the church at Corinth.

> *Now I beseech you, brethren, by the name of our Lord Jesus Christ, that ye all speak the same thing, and that there be no divisions among you; but that ye be perfectly joined together in the same mind and in the same judgment.*
> 1 Corinthians 1:10

Paul appealed to the church at Corinth, he did not command them. He gave them spiritual guidance as the founder, but never lorded it over them. The appointment of the elders by the apostle worked well.

In the churches there were always multiple elders appointed, and there is no record of one having greater authority or a higher title. The elders were equal. We need to consider these concepts together. We saw the importance of having more than one elder earlier, so that all the flock could be attended to and none would be overlooked. This is a major problem in the Church of the 20th century. Another tremendous advantage of having multiple elders is that it keeps the church from straying. Following is an example:

A senior pastor can say to his assistant pastors, "I believe we are to stop going out to preach the gospel. This is not the 20th-century way of sharing the gospel. We will advertise a lot and have some special programs to draw people in. This is what the Lord seems to be speaking to me." Now, whether the other pastors agree or not, the senior pastor is in control and often will do what he believes is right. If you're a newly hired associate who has transferred from another area, you may be reluctant to challenge this decision, fearing that you may find yourself out on the street.

I have found from experience in dealing with many churches that because of the predominance of the pastoral ministry, the evangelistic thrust of a church is often neglected, as seen in the above example. The pastoral ministry usually is the only one of the fivefold ministries functioning in a church. Thus, pastoral and teaching programs abound. Sometimes it is an evangelist who is the senior pastor, then evangelism becomes everything for this church, while pastoring suffers.

Let's return to our example and see what would happen if there were several elders, each having the same authority, and one elder proposed such a plan. If the foundation had been properly laid and the fivefold ministry were intact, then this church and these elders would not be easily sidetracked from its Great Commission, to go *out* and preach the gospel. One of the other elders might come forward with the Word of God to say, "The Word of God says this..., therefore we cannot adopt your plan; parts of it are unscriptural. We must continue to go out and preach the gospel as Jesus did and as the apostles and disciples were commanded to do." With the Word of God as the authority and as other elders consent to the word, this plan (of the devil) to get the church off track would be overthrown.

A good, sound scriptural idea or activity, such as prayer meetings, needs to be carried out. With multiple and equal eldership, the good ideas will more likely be implemented and the bad ideas and unscriptural ones will be tossed aside, while all the time the elders weigh the motives of their hearts. This is the process through which a church stays in the will of God.

The unscrupulous motives of one pastor cannot be allowed to run the church off its mark. A moral breakdown of one pastor can be handled better in a system whereby he will not be allowed to continue to minister in a pastoral capacity. Other elders with equal power can approach him. If one of the elders were to continue in a state of sin, the apostle could be called back to set it straight.

In summary, the government and spiritual rule over the Church has been sorely overlooked. We Christians have naively accepted the traditional church format whereby one pastor presides over the congregation. This present-day system of church rule has sidetracked the Church and is rendering it powerless. A church was meant to be governed by a plurality of elders, all having equal authority and having been set in place by the apostles and prophets. Each local church is to be autonomous, with the elders and others in the fivefold ministry ruling over the church. This is a theocracy whereby God can rule and direct His people. Yes, Jesus is standing outside the door of many churches, looking for a church with a sound foundation, a church that He wills to endue with Holy Spirit power.

Conclusion

I am looking forward to the Lord's return. When the Lord does come back for His church, I don't believe the devil will be able to mock the Lord and say, "See, You had to come and get Your children because they could not stand up to me. They are weak and scared and run from me." No, this is not the way I believe it will be. The Church will be a powerful force throughout the world, having aggressively advanced the Kingdom of God to the uttermost ends of the world. In a brief period of time the whole world will be known either as sheep or goats. Either they will have received Jesus as the Christ or rejected him.

The only way this can happen is that in the last days there will be a tremendous pouring out of the

Holy Spirit upon a people prepared to do the works of Christ. This will be the case when the Church has a sound foundation, a foundation laid by apostles and prophets who built upon Christ. It will be a Church with all the giftings of the fivefold ministry at work and with all the gifts that the Lord has given to each Christian in operation. This Church will have Christians who have matured into true disciples and have been molded into a mighty army to confront the devil head on. This body of believers, this mighty army, will be endued with a supernatural power as they go forth proclaiming the good news, healing the sick and casting out demons.

Now he that has an ear, let him hear what the Spirit says. The present-day Church is steeped in sin. Many church leaders have not heeded the Word of God and have turned their backs on God's gifts to the Church: the apostles, prophets and evangelists. Furthermore, they refuse to repent. The Lord is about to do a new thing. Out of the stones, if need be, Jesus Christ will build His Church according to His word. You will know this Church because it will be a people endued with power. Be prepared to come out and separate yourself.

Epilogue

It is hoped that this book has been a challenge for you. However, the next step you take will be the most difficult. Where do you go from here?

If you need help or have additional questions regarding the foundation of the Church, apostles and prophets, the making of disciples, church ministries, or any other topics mentioned in this book, please feel free to correspond.

Write to:

> A Church of Power Ministries
> Attn. Don Faix
> P.O. Box 16102
> Rochester, NY 14616

To order additional copies of
A Church of Power Is Emerging
send check or money order for
$7.95 plus $2.00 postage and handling to

A Church of Power Ministries
P.O. Box 16102
Rochester, NY 14616

or call
Destiny Image Publishers
1-800-722-6774